MAXnotes®

William Shakespeare's

Hamlet

Text by
Joanne K. Miller
(M.A., University of Northern Iowa)
Department of English
Harrison High School
West Lafayette, Indiana

Illustrations by
Karen Pica

 Research & Education Association
Dr. M. Fogiel, Director

D0837558

MAXnotes® for
HAMLET

Year 2002 Printing

Printed in the United States of America

Library of Congress Control Number 99-74574

International Standard Book Number 0-87891-952-X

What **MAXnotes**® *Will Do for You*

This book is intended to help you absorb the essential contents and features of William Shakespeare's *Hamlet* and to help you gain a thorough understanding of the work. Our book has been designed to do this more quickly and effectively than any other study guide.

For best results, this **MAXnotes** book should be used as a companion to the actual work, not instead of it. The interaction between the two will greatly benefit you.

To help you in your studies, this book presents the most up-to-date interpretations of every section of the actual work, followed by questions and fully explained answers that will enable you to analyze the material critically. The questions also will help you to test your understanding of the work and will prepare you for discussions and exams.

Meaningful illustrations are included to further enhance your understanding and enjoyment of the literary work. The illustrations are designed to place you into the mood and spirit of the work's settings.

The **MAXnotes** also include summaries, character lists, explanations of plot, and section-by-section analyses. A biography of the author and discussion of the work's historical context will help you put this literary piece into the proper framework of what is taking place.

The use of this study guide will save you the hours of preparation time that would ordinarily be required to arrive at a complete grasp of this work of literature. You will be well-prepared for classroom discussions, homework, and exams. The guidelines that are included for writing papers and reports on various topics will prepare you for any added work which may be assigned.

The **MAXnotes** will take your grades "to the max."

Dr. Max Fogiel
Program Director

Contents

> **Each scene includes List of Characters, Summary, Analysis, Study Questions and Answers, and Suggested Essay Topics.**

MAXnotes® are simply the best – but don't just take our word for it...

A Glance at Some of the Characters

Hamlet

Ghost of Hamlet's Father

Claudius

Gertrude

Ophelia

Laertes

Polonius

SECTION ONE

Introduction

The Life and Work of William Shakespeare

Details about William Shakespeare's life are sketchy, mostly mere surmise based upon court or other clerical records. His parents, John and Mary (Arden), were married about 1557; she was of the landed gentry, he a yeoman—a glover and commodities merchant. By 1568, John had risen through the ranks of town government and held the position of high bailiff, similar to mayor. William, the eldest son, was born in 1564, probably on April 23, several days before his baptism on April 26, 1564. That Shakespeare also died on April 23, 52 years later, may have resulted in the adoption of this birthdate.

William no doubt attended the local grammar school in Stratford where his parents lived, and would have studied primarily Latin rhetoric, logic, and literature [Barnet, viii]. At age 18 (1582), William married Anne Hathaway, a local farmer's daughter eight years his senior. Their first daughter (Susanna) was born six months later (1583), and twins Judith and Hamnet were born in 1585.

Shakespeare's life can be divided into three periods: the first 20 years in Stratford, which include his schooling, early marriage, and fatherhood; the next 25 years as an actor and playwright in London; and the last five in retirement back in Stratford where he enjoyed moderate wealth gained from his theatrical successes. The years linking the first two periods are marked by a lack of information about Shakespeare, and are often referred to as the "dark years"; the transition from active work into retirement was gradual and cannot be precisely dated [Boyce, 587].

John Shakespeare had suffered financial reverses from William's teen years until well into the height of the playwright's popularity and success. In 1596, John Shakespeare was granted a coat of arms, almost certainly purchased by William, who the next year bought a sizable house in Stratford. By the time of his death, William had substantial properties, both professional and personal, which he bestowed on his theatrical associates and his family (primarily his daughter Susanna, having rewritten his will one month before his death to protect his assets from Judith's new husband, Thomas Quiney, who ran afoul of church doctrine and public esteem before and after the marriage) [Boyce, 529].

Shakespeare probably left school at 15, which was the norm, and took some sort of job, especially since this was the period of his father's financial difficulty. Numerous references in his plays suggest that William may have in fact worked for his father, thereby gaining specialized knowledge [Boyce, 587].

At some point during the "dark years," Shakespeare began his career with a London theatrical company—perhaps in 1589—for he was already an actor and playwright of some note in 1592. Shakespeare apparently wrote and acted for Pembroke's Men, as well as numerous others, in particular Strange's Men, which later became the Chamberlain's Men, with whom he remained for the rest of his career.

When, in 1592, the Plague closed the theaters for about two years, Shakespeare turned to writing book-length narrative poetry. Most notable were "Venus and Adonis" and "The Rape of Lucrece," both of which were dedicated to the Earl of Southampton, whom scholars accept as Shakespeare's friend and benefactor despite a lack of documentation. During this same period, Shakespeare was writing his sonnets, which are more likely signs of the time's fashion rather than actual love poems detailing any particular relationship. He returned to play writing when theaters reopened in 1594, and published no more poetry. His sonnets were published without his consent in 1609, shortly before his retirement.

Amid all of his success, Shakespeare suffered the loss of his only son, Hamnet, who died in 1596 at the age of 11. But Shakespeare's career continued unabated, and in London in 1599, he became one of the partners in the new Globe Theater [Boyce, 589], built by the Chamberlain's Men. This group was a remarkable assemblage of "excellent actors who were also business partners and close personal friends . . . [including] Richard Burbage . . . [who] all worked together as equals . . . " [Chute, 131].

When Queen Elizabeth died in 1603 and was succeeded by her cousin King James of Scotland, the Chamberlain's Men was renamed the King's Men, and Shakespeare's productivity and popularity continued uninterrupted. He invested in London real estate and, one year away from retirement, purchased a second theater, the Blackfriars Gatehouse, in partnership with his fellow actors. His final play was *Henry VIII*, two years before his death in 1616.

Incredibly, most of Shakespeare's plays had never been published in anything except pamphlet form, and were simply extant as acting scripts stored at the Globe. Only the efforts of two of Shakespeare's company, John Heminges and Henry Condell, preserved his 36 plays (minus *Pericles*, the thirty-seventh) [Barnet, xvii] in the First Folio. Heminges and Condell published the plays, they said, "only to keep the memory of so worthy a friend and fellow alive as was our Shakespeare" [Chute, 133]. Theater scripts were not regarded as literary works of art, but only the basis for the performance. Plays were a popular form of entertainment for all layers of society in Shakespeare's time, which perhaps explains why Hamlet feels compelled to instruct the traveling Players on the fine points of acting, urging them not "to split the ears of the groundlings," nor "speak no more than is set down for them."

Present copies of Shakespeare's plays have, in some cases, been reconstructed in part from scripts written down by various members of an acting company who performed particular roles. Shakespeare's plays, like those of many of the actors who also were playwrights, belonged to the acting company. The performance, rather than the script, was what concerned the author, for that was how his play would become popular—and how the company, in which many actors were shareholders, would make money.

William Shakespeare died on April 23, 1616, and was buried two days later in the chancel of Holy Trinity Church where he had been baptized exactly 52 years earlier.

Historical Background

There is general agreement about the sources for Shakespeare's *Hamlet*. About 400 years prior to the Elizabethan version, Saxo Grammaticus told a similar tale in his *Historia Danica* (c. 1200). About 15 years before Shakespeare's version, Francois de Belleforest adopted the essential story in his *Histoires Tragiques* (1576), a popular collection of tales in French. Both of these sources survive as literary manuscripts.

However, most critics believe that another source, the so-called *Ur-Hamlet*, is the version most directly responsible for many of the elements which Shakespeare incorporated into his play. Although no written version of this precursor exists, and historians can only work backwards from documents which mention the *Ur-Hamlet*, it is believed that this play, probably written by Thomas Kyd, was acted in 1594 by the Lord Admiral's Men and the Lord Chamberlain's Men, the latter of which company Shakespeare belonged to.

While the earlier versions included similar elements to Shakespeare's Hamlet (the hero's love interest, fratricide, feigned madness, adultery, spies, and revenge), only Kyd's version includes the Ghost who seeks revenge. In fact, Kyd's famous play, *The Spanish Tragedy*, includes other elements which Shakespeare seems to have incorporated into *Hamlet*: "a procrastinating protagonist who berates himself for talking instead of acting and who dies as he achieves his revenge; . . . a play within a play, a heroine whose love is opposed by her family, and another woman who becomes insane and commits suicide" [Boyce, 238–239]. However, if Kyd did not author the *Ur-Hamlet*, both he and Shakespeare may have borrowed from this same "Ur-" source for their respective works.

There are other sources, both real and fictional, which may have contributed to Shakespeare's version, including women who killed themselves for love (1577), and a barber who confessed (in 1538) to murdering an Italian duke by putting lotion in his ears. In the second instance, Gonzago was the name of the plotter, rather than of the victim, as in Shakespeare's "mousetrap."

Hamlet was most likely performed in 1600, almost exactly at the midpoint of his writing career, which had begun as early as 1588 with *The Comedy of Errors*, and ended as late as 1613 with *Henry VIII*. Shakespeare's allusions to his *Julius Caesar* (1599) in *Hamlet*, and references by other playwrights in late 1600 (John Marston's *Antonio's Revenge*) place the performance of *Hamlet* fairly precisely. However, the Player's dialogue with Hamlet about the child actors is a direct reference to actual competition between rival theater companies in the spring of 1601; perhaps this scene was added later, or perhaps Shakespeare used Marston's play as a source rather than the other way around [Boyce, 239–240].

The first performance is held to be that of the Chamberlain's Men, in 1600 or 1601. Shakespeare's longtime theatrical associate, Richard Burbage, was the first Hamlet; tradition has it that Shakespeare himself played the Ghost in the original production.

The first publication of *Hamlet* was in 1603 in a quarto edition known as *Q1*, and generally regarded as reconstructed from actors' memories who had performed in the play. In 1604, *Q2* was published, most likely from Shakespeare's own manuscript; however, passages were edited out of *Q2* because they were politically sensitive or simply dated. Between 1611 and 1637, *Q3*, *Q4*, and *Q5* were published as reprints of each foregoing edition.

The first folio edition of Shakespeare's plays (1623), known as *F*, contained *Hamlet* and seems to have used *Q2* as its source. Significant differences include the restoration of the passages cut from *Q2*, the modernization of words thought by the editors to be out of date, and inclusion of some lines which seem to be actors' ad libs rather than Shakespeare's text. Modern editors usually use *Q2* because it is closest to Shakespeare's text, but also because it has the restored passages and other minor improvements [Boyce, 240].

Hamlet is regarded as one of Shakespeare's finest tragedies, along with *Othello*, *King Lear*, and *Macbeth*, all of which followed in the next five or six years (along with four other major plays). Over the years it has been the most often performed of Shakespeare's plays, and has been filmed at least 25 times and televised five times [Boyce, 241]. Most performances use an abridged text, since the original could take four to five hours. Beginning in 1775 with Sarah Siddons, women began playing the title role, including, in 1971, Judith Anderson at age 73 [Boyce, 240].

Master List of Characters

Barnardo, Francisco, Mercellus—*sentinels; officers in King of Denmark's army*

Horatio—*Prince Hamlet's friend and confidante; fellow-student at Wittenberg*

Ghost—*of dead King of Denmark, Prince Hamlet's father; brother of new King, husband of Gertrude*

Claudius—*brother of dead King of Denmark; now King, and new husband of Queen Gertrude, Prince Hamlet's mother*

Gertrude—*Prince Hamlet's mother, widow of former King, now wife to Claudius, new King.*

Polonius—*King Claudius' advisor; father to Laertes and Ophelia*

Reynaldo—*Polonius' servant, sent to Paris to spy on Laertes*

Laertes—*son to Polonius, brother to Ophelia; friend to Hamlet*

Prince Hamlet—*son of the late King, and of Queen Gertrude; nephew-stepson to King Claudius*

Voltemand and Cornelius—*messengers to King of Norway from Claudius*

Ophelia—*daughter to Polonius, sister to Laertes, beloved of Hamlet*

Rosencrantz and Guildenstern—*fellow students of Hamlet at Wittenberg; sent with Hamlet to England by Claudius to murder Hamlet*

Osric—*messenger who summons Hamlet to duel with Laertes*

The Players—*actors (adults) who formerly performed in the city, and who are now traveling because of the rising popularity of companies of child actors*

Grave diggers—*two clowns (rustics) who are disinterring an old grave in order to make way for a new burial, Ophelia*

Priest—*Doctor of Divinity (church official) presiding at Ophelia's funeral*

Fortinbras—*Prince of Norway whose father was killed by Hamlet's father; assumes throne of Denmark at play's end*

Ambassador—*from England, reporting to Claudius*

Summary of the Play

Prince Hamlet of Denmark is urged by his father's Ghost to avenge his murder at the hands of the dead king's brother, now King Claudius; to make matters worse, Claudius has married the widow, Hamlet's mother, Queen Gertrude. Denmark is under threat of invasion from young Fortinbras, who seeks to regain lands lost to Hamlet's father by Fortinbras' father. Claudius sends word to the King of Norway (Fortinbras' uncle) to curb Fortinbras' aggression. In the meantime, Hamlet feigns madness with his family and friends, including his beloved, Ophelia, sister to Laertes and daughter to Polonius. Both Polonius and Laertes warn Ophelia against Hamlet's amorous advances. Polonius believes Hamlet's "madness" to be love sickness. Laertes is given permission to return to his studies in Paris.

Claudius directs Gertrude to try to learn the cause of Hamlet's odd behavior; they suspect it is the old king's death and their own recent marriage. Meantime, Claudius and Polonius eavesdrop on Ophelia and Hamlet, who spurns her and appears mad. The King reveals to Polonius his plan to send Hamlet to England with Rosencrantz and Guildenstern.

Hamlet seizes the opportunity presented by a traveling troupe of players to expose the King's guilt with a "play within a play." Soon after, Hamlet delays killing Claudius because the King is at prayer, and Hamlet does not wish to send him to heaven instead of hell. When Gertrude meets with Hamlet as Claudius has directed, Polonius hides behind the arras in Gertrude's room to eavesdrop on the conversation. Hamlet, suspecting the interloper is Claudius, stabs and kills Polonius.

When Polonius' body is discovered, Claudius summons Hamlet and tells him he must sail to England for his own safety; Rosencrantz and Guildenstern accompany Hamlet, carrying letters to the English, threatening war unless they kill Hamlet. Hamlet eventually escapes, returns to Denmark, and is met by Horatio. Ophelia has gone insane after Hamlet's departure and her father's death. Laertes returns and vows to avenge Polonius' death. Claudius contrives a fencing match between Hamlet and Laertes, during which Hamlet is to be injured with a poisoned sword tip and poisoned with a drink, thus assuring his death. When news arrives that Ophelia has drowned herself, Laertes is grief stricken. Hamlet and Horatio happen upon the burial site and funeral cortege; Hamlet tries to fight Laertes but is restrained.

Hamlet tells Horatio that he rewrote the papers carried by Rosencrantz and Guildenstern, and that the letters now call for their own deaths. Osric invites Hamlet to the duel with Laertes; Claudius has supposedly bet on Hamlet to win. Gertrude mistakenly drinks from the cup poisoned by Claudius for Hamlet, and dies; Laertes wounds Hamlet with the poisoned sword, and then Hamlet wounds Laertes when they accidentally exchange swords. When Laertes reveals the conspiracy, Hamlet wounds the King and forces the poisoned drink upon him. Laertes and Hamlet reconcile, and Laertes dies; Hamlet prevents Horatio from drinking the poison so that he can live to tell the truth. Hamlet names as his successor young Fortinbras, who arrives and orders Hamlet buried with all dignity.

Estimated Reading Time

Given a text with abundant and helpful footnotes, an average student should expect to spend at least an hour per act on the first read through; subsequent readings should take less time, as the language becomes more familiar. Certainly a five hour stretch is not advised; probably a few scenes at a time, or perhaps an entire act, would be a comfortable portion for an average reader. Since there are five acts with a total of 20 scenes, the student could expect to spend at least five hours in perhaps six to eight sessions.

Act I

Act I, Scene 1

New Characters:

Barnardo, Francisco, and Marcellus: *sentinels*

Horatio: *Hamlet's close friend and confidante*

Ghost: *of Hamlet's father, the former King of Denmark*

Summary

Just after the striking of twelve, Francisco is relieved of his watch by Barnardo and Marcellus, who have entreated Horatio to stand with them this night to witness the reappearance of the dead king's apparition. The Ghost appears and disappears twice but does not speak to the four, who decide to tell Hamlet in the morning. They note that a Ghost often portends grave events, and believe the King's Ghost is related to the impending war with young Fortinbras of Norway, who seeks to regain the lands his late father lost in battle with the dead King of Denmark, Hamlet's father.

Analysis

The Ghost of Hamlet's father appears for the second time to Barnardo, Marcellus, and Francisco, who are this time accompanied by Horatio, Hamlet's trusted friend and fellow student—perhaps his scholarly title lending credence to the apparition. When they persuade Hamlet to witness the sight, the third time is the charm; the heretofore silent Ghost speaks—but only to Hamlet, whom it has drawn apart, not to the others.

Thus begins one of the play's recurrent motifs: indirection and deception. The various witnesses have different interpretations of the events. The officers assume "that this portentous figure / Comes armed through our watch so like the King / That was and is the question of these wars" with young Fortinbras. Hamlet, however, learns that his father's Ghost wants him, "If thou didst ever thy dear father love— . . . [to] / Revenge his foul and most unnatural murder."

Act I, Scene 2

New Characters:

Claudius, King of Denmark: *Prince Hamlet's uncle and stepfather*

Gertrude, the Queen: *Hamlet's mother*

Polonius: *the King's advisor*

Laertes: *son to Polonius*

Prince Hamlet: *son of the late King and Queen Gertrude*

Voltemand and Cornelius: *messengers to King of Norway*

Summary

King Claudius announces that, despite his grief over his brother's recent death, he has taken Gertrude to wife. He also informs the court of young Fortinbras' aggression, and assigns Voltemand and Cornelius to deliver a dispatch to the King of Norway (Fortinbras' uncle) urging that he restrain his nephew. Laertes asks the King's permission to return to France, which he left to attend the coronation. The King grants the request, being assured that Polonius also assents. The King and Queen then urge Hamlet to cease his mourning, and to abandon his plan to return to his studies in Wittenberg; Hamlet agrees.

Everyone departs, leaving Hamlet alone to lament his mother's hasty remarriage to a man less worthy than her first husband, Hamlet's father. Horatio, Marcellus, and Barnardo enter and tell

Hamlet of the Ghostly apparition; he vows to watch with them that night and speak to it.

Analysis

King Claudius and his new bride worry over Hamlet's odd behavior; Gertrude correctly guesses that he is upset over his father's death and their "o'erhasty" marriage, a surmise which suggests that the queen feels some twinge of guilt over her recent actions. The royal couple press Hamlet to stay in Denmark at court, and not return to his studies in Wittenberg.

Claudius' motives are, of course, ulterior: to spy on Hamlet in order to learn the true cause of his madness, again suggesting that Claudius has some cause to fear retribution from his nephew/son. Perhaps incredibly, Hamlet agrees to their request to remain, even before he vows to avenge his father's death. Why he would stay in an environment he finds uncomfortable and distasteful is a puzzle, unless we assume filial obedience as his overriding motive. More likely, however, this turn of events is another instance of the inexorable workings of fate, bringing together all the "actors" in some cosmic drama, as later scenes will bear witness.

Act I, Scene 3

New Character:

Ophelia: *daughter to Polonius; sister to Laertes*

Summary

Laertes meets Ophelia to say his farewells before returning to France. He warns her to beware of Hamlet's trifling with her, and urges her to remain chaste. Ophelia agrees to heed his advice, while urging him to obey it as well. Polonius enters and counsels Laertes, who departs. Polonius also warns Ophelia of Hamlet's amorous intentions, and finally instructs her to avoid him altogether. She assents.

Analysis

This scene presents tender, if somewhat humorous, dialogue between sister and brother, father and son, and father and daughter. Buried in the conversation, however, is the undercurrent of honesty vs. deceit, love vs. betrayal, reality vs. appearances—all themes which recur throughout the play. Both Laertes and Polonius show great solicitude for Ophelia's welfare, and she exhibits demure obedience to their advice, born of wider experience of the world than her own.

Act I, Scene 4

Summary

Hamlet, Horatio, and Marcellus wait just after midnight to see the Ghost. It appears, and beckons to Hamlet, who follows it. Horatio and Marcellus go after them.

Analysis

First Horatio, and now Hamlet, have been brought to verify the appearance and identity of the Ghost. Hamlet appears resolute as he follows the beckoning apparition, though the others advise against it. His courage and resolution in this short scene are in sharp contrast to his apparent attitude in later scenes as he struggles with the issue of revenge.

Act I, Scene 5

Summary

The Ghost of his father tells Hamlet that he was murdered by poison poured into his ear by Claudius. The Ghost urges Hamlet to avenge him, but to leave judgment of his mother to heaven. As the Ghost leaves, Hamlet swears to remember his father. Hamlet refuses to divulge the conversation to Horatio and Marcellus when they appear, and the Ghost reappears, repeatedly crying for them to "Swear" not to tell what they have seen. Hamlet also instructs

them not to reveal the truth if he appears to be acting "odd" later on, and they finally so swear. Hamlet laments his appointed role as avenger of so great a wrong.

Analysis

That the Ghost swears the soldiers to secrecy puts an extra burden on Hamlet. His mission to avenge his father may require him to do things which will appear odd or, as it turns out, insane, to onlookers. But the men who could explain his behavior are sworn not to reveal its cause. Further, Hamlet is sworn to leave his mother's judgment to heaven. Thus, Hamlet is admonished against releasing anger at his mother, yet obliged to pursue revenge against Claudius in ways that may seem illogical and unwarranted. His resulting mental anguish seems inevitable.

Study Questions

1. Why does the Ghost of Hamlet's father appear but not speak to the officers on sentinel duty?

2. What do Ghostly apparitions usually portend, according to these witnesses?

3. What is the content of the dispatches Claudius has sent with Voltemand and Cornelius to the King of Norway?

4. In his soliloquy, what are Hamlet's reasons for objecting to his mother's remarriage?

5. What advice does Laertes give to Ophelia as he says farewell to her prior to his departure for Paris?

6. What advice does she give Laertes in return?

7. What is the thrust of the advice Polonius gives Laertes as his son prepares to leave?

8. What does Polonius instruct Ophelia to do regarding Hamlet?

9. What does the apparition tell Hamlet?

10. What two-part oath does Hamlet extract from his companions following the encounter with the Ghost?

Answers

1. Horatio believes he has offended it by demanding that it speak, and Marcellus believes his threat of violence was ill-

conceived on a spirit, which is "as the air, invulnerable." Horatio and Marcellus also recall the folk wisdom that the cock's crowing sends spirits to their "confine." Additionally, in the season just before Christmas, the cock crows all night, and "no spirit dare stir abroad . . . So hallowed and so gracious is that time."

2. Horatio remembers similar Ghostly appearances were reported shortly before Julius Caesar's fall, and believes the Ghost to be a "precurse of feared events" to Denmark. "Or if thou hast uphoarded in thy life / Extorted treasure in the womb of earth, / For which, they say, you spirits oft walk in death," suggests that Horatio acknowledges that the apparition may not have any particular relevance to the current political situation.

3. Claudius wants Norway, uncle to Fortinbras, "to suppress [Fortinbras'] further gait herein, in that the levies, / The lists, and full proportions are all made / Out of [Norway's] subject. . . . "

4. Hamlet feels the marriage was too soon after his father's death; he can't see how his mother could have so soon forgotten her love and devotion to her husband. Furthermore, he feels his uncle is "no more like my father / Than I to Hercules." He believes his mother has violated English canon law, which held that marriage with a deceased brother's widow was incestuous [Hubler, 45].

5. Laertes tells his sister to regard Hamlet's attentions as trifling, toying, temporary diversions of youthful fancy. Also, he reminds her that Hamlet, as heir apparent, is subject to the will of Denmark; he may say he loves her now, but if the state requires it, he would have to marry otherwise. If in the meantime she loses her virtue to him, it will be for nothing. "Be wary then; best safety lies in fear. . . . "

6. She urges him to take his own advice, and not be like a pastor who instructs his flock how to achieve heaven but who "Himself the primrose path of dalliance treads . . . "

7. It is wide ranging, but urges moderation, integrity, thrift, and

"above all, to thine own self be true . . . Thou canst not then be false to any man."

8. Polonius says Ophelia is a "baby" to have believed Hamlet's "tenders of affection," which are "mere implorators [solicitors] . . . [meant] to beguile." He commands her to "Be something scanter of your maiden presence. . . . [nor] slander any moment leisure / As to give words or talk with the Lord Hamlet."

9. The Ghost reveals the circumstances of his murder and charges Hamlet to avenge his death, but to "Leave [thy mother] to heaven" and to her own conscience.

10. Hamlet makes them swear never to tell what they have seen that night, and never, "How strange or odd some'er I bear myself (As I perchance hereafter shall think meet To put an antic disposition on), / That you, at such times seeing me, never shall . . . note / That you know aught of me. . . . " In other words, he makes them swear not to reveal that his madness is merely put on.

Suggested Essay Topics

1. Contrast the attitudes towards the death of the old King as expressed by Claudius and Hamlet.

2. Compare the advice given to Ophelia by Laertes and that given by Polonius.

Act II

Act II, Scene 1

New Character:

Reynaldo: *Polonius' servant*

Summary

Polonius sends Reynaldo to Paris to spy on Laertes, instructing him to use delicate indirection to learn of Laertes' behavior from "other Danskers [who] are in Paris." After Reynaldo leaves, Ophelia enters, distressed, and tells her father that Hamlet has just approached her with "his doublet all unbraced, / No hat upon his head, his stockings fouled, / Ungartered, and down-gyved to his ankle." She says he "held [her] hard" by the wrist, studied her silently for several moments, sighed "piteous and profound," and then left her. Polonius believes Hamlet is lovesick because Ophelia has shunned him, and modifies his earlier suspicion that Hamlet meant only to trifle with Ophelia. Polonius and Ophelia depart to inform Claudius of this news.

Analysis

Scene 1 shows Ophelia to be a naive young girl who trusts her father's judgment and is obedient to his will. Polonius' tedious instructions to Reynaldo echo his earlier advice to both Ophelia and Laertes, and foreshadow his behavior in Scene 2. When Reynaldo asks why he is being sent to spy on Laertes, Polonius' justification

is so circuitous even he loses track of what he was saying: "What was I about to say? By the mass, I was about to say something! Where did I leave?"

Act II, Scene 2

New Characters:

Rosencrantz and Guildenstern: *longtime friends and former schoolmates of Hamlet*

Voltemand and Cornelius: *sent by Claudius as ambassadors to King of Norway*

The Players: *traveling actors hired to perform at the castle*

Summary

King Claudius and Queen Gertrude receive Rosencrantz and Guildenstern, childhood friends of Hamlet, who agree to visit him and seek the cause of Hamlet's "transformation." Polonius enters to announce the arrival of Voltemand and Cornelius from Norway, and to say that he believes he has found the "very cause of Hamlet's lunacy." However, he delays revealing the information until the ambassadors have been heard, although Claudius does "long to hear" of it. Voltemand and Cornelius report that the ailing King of Norway, having discovered that young Fortinbras intended to attack Denmark rather than Poland, has redirected Fortinbras' aggression against Poland and now asks safe passage through Denmark for Norway's armies. Claudius agrees to consider the request.

Finally, when Polonius begins his story, he is so discursive that Gertrude pleads, "More matter, with less art." He then begins to read them the letter he took from Ophelia. Impatient, Gertrude interrupts with "Came this from Hamlet to her?" But Polonius controls the pacing with, "Good madam, stay awhile. I will be faithful." When Claudius asks how Ophelia has received Hamlet's love, Polonius takes the opportunity to cite his own virtues as a watchful father, who prudently checked and advised his daughter. To Claudius' query, "Do you think 'tis [love sickness]?", Polonius confidently answers, "Hath there been such a time . . . That I have positively said, '"Tis so,' When it proved otherwise? . . . I will find / Where truth is hid, though it were hid indeed Within the center." He even stakes his career as advisor on it if he is wrong: "Let me be no assistant for a state / But keep a farm and carters."

Having given a very dramatic account of Hamlet's love sickness, Polonius arranges that Claudius and he will eavesdrop on a contrived conversation between Ophelia and Hamlet to prove his suspicions. The royal pair exit quickly as Hamlet enters, reading a book.

Polonius and Hamlet have a brief conversation full of non sequiturs and punned insults, which confirms Polonius' opinion regarding the prince's madness. The old man leaves when Rosencrantz and Guildenstern enter. Hamlet suggests that in coming to Denmark they have come to a prison, and finally gets them to admit that they have been "sent for." He even guesses their assignment: to discover why he has "of late . . . lost all [his] mirth . . ." so that "Man delights [him not], nor woman neither." The pair tell Hamlet that they have persuaded a traveling company of tragedians to perform for the court. As the players enter, Hamlet confides to his friends that he is only feigning his madness, despite what his "uncle-father and aunt-mother" believe: "I am but mad north-northwest: when the wind is southerly I know a hawk from a handsaw."

Polonius enters to announce the arrival of the players, whom Hamlet warmly welcomes. After he has one of the players recite a section from Aeneas' tale to Dido detailing Pyrrhus' murder of Priam, Hamlet secretly asks the actor if the players could present *The Murder of Gonzago* the next night, including a short insert "of some dozen or sixteen lines" which Hamlet will provide. The actor agrees.

When all have left, Hamlet contrasts his own seeming lack of passion in avenging his father's death to the actor's impassioned performance for imaginary characters the player does not even know. Hamlet resolves to test whether his father's Ghost is a devil sent to damn him by staging a play which presents a murder similar to his father's. Claudius' reaction to the scenes will reveal whether or not he is guilty.

Analysis

The lengthy second scene slows the lively pace which was characteristic of Act I, which had five fairly brief scenes, followed by the brisk first scene of Act II. This slowdown allows Shakespeare to establish beyond doubt that Claudius is guilty of the King's murder, and to begin to explore Hamlet's tortured mental state, caught between love, grief, and vengeance. The loyalty of Hamlet's friends, Rosencrantz and Guildenstern, is turned against him by his parents; yet, when Hamlet presses them, they give up the charade and admit their mission. They have even arranged the theatrical interlude because they know Hamlet was "wont to take . . . delight in" their performances. Their obvious affection for Hamlet creates a problem for the reader when, in Act V, Scene 2, Hamlet reveals that he has forged the letters which will result in their deaths. He will justify his actions, saying essentially that his friends got caught in the middle, between him and Claudius; that their "own insinuation" (meddling) has brought about their defeat.

The conversation about the established adult acting companies versus the increasingly popular child actors was not only topical for Shakespeare's audiences, but is also dramatically integral to the intergenerational motif of the play: the youth rising up to supplant their elders. Furthermore, the motif of illusion vs. reality which pervades the play is reinforced here with the several mentions of young boys playing the parts of women, also a timely reference. In addition, the suggestion that women are weaker or otherwise inferior is a recurrent motif: "frailty, thy name is woman—"; "O most pernicious woman!"; " . . . it is such a kind of gaingiving as would perhaps trouble a woman."

Voltemand and Cornelius bring news of Norway's curbing of Fortinbras' revenge aimed at Denmark, reinforcing another of the recurring motifs in this play: parents vs. children, and its flipside, children (sons, in this case) seeking to avenge their fathers' deaths. Fortinbras' father had lost his lands to Hamlet's father in the recent war, and young Fortinbras plans to regain them by attack. His uncle, now King of Norway, intercedes and sets him against Poland. Hamlet and Fortinbras are both dispossessed heirs to the throne; in Act V, Scene 2, Hamlet will give his "dying voice" to Fortinbras' accession to the throne of Denmark, and Fortinbras will eulogize Hamlet as "a soldier" and "most royal." Thus, out of the chaos, we are assured order will be restored, and power passed into capable and worthy hands.

Hamlet's inane conversations with both Polonius and with Rosencrantz and Guildenstern are riddled with vulgar innuendoes, which foreshadows his scenes with Ophelia and Gertrude. The discrepancy between outer appearances and inner qualities is thus manifested once again; Hamlet even states this theme directly in his conversation with Gertrude, when he tells her that her trespass "will but skin and film the ulcerous place / Whiles rank corruption, mining all within, / Infects unseen." That Hamlet's madness is merely pretense in this scene is suggested by his remark as Polonius departs ("These tedious old fools!") and by his disclosure that his parents are "deceived" about his madness.

When Polonius announces the arrival of the players, Hamlet remarks to Guildenstern and Rosencrantz "That great baby you see there is not yet out of his swaddling clouts;" to which Rosencrantz counters, " . . . they say an old man is twice a child." Clearly Hamlet does not respect Polonius, despite his politically important position. Throughout the play, Polonius appears as arrogant, foolish, self-important, and unaware that others find him amusing, if not tedious. In proclaiming his own skills as an advisor and father, he has apparently forgotten that he was earlier forced to admit his change of mind, abandoning his assumption that Hamlet meant to trifle with Ophelia: "I am sorry that with better heed and judgment I had not quoted him. . . . By heaven, it is as proper to our age / To cast beyond ourselves in our opinions / As it is common for the younger sort / To lack discretion."

Hamlet continues to bait the king's advisor with allusions to Jeptha, a Biblical king who sacrificed his daughter, implying a parallel to Polonius' "loosing" Ophelia to Hamlet to verify his madness. That Hamlet understands the motives of those around him to be duplicitous is becoming increasingly clear, and that Hamlet's madness is merely pretense, increasingly certain. If he is not mad, we may perhaps assume that his actions—and his inaction—are conscious and calculated.

Many critics have argued the issue of Hamlet's inaction—that is, his delay in avenging his father's death. The prince frequently laments his procrastination, contrasting himself to Fortinbras (who must be restrained from his planned vengeance for his father's death) and to Pyrrhus (who takes sporting delight in "mincing" Priam—merely the father of Paris, the actual murderer of Pyrrhus' father, Achilles). What is it that holds Hamlet back? Probably no one theory will encompass the body of evidence to be found in the entire work, but several major interpretations have been supported over the centuries by critics.

It is possible that Hamlet really had no opportunity to kill Claudius, with the exception of the time he found him at prayer. Not wishing to kill Claudius when the king's soul and conscience were clear, Hamlet delays. Ironically, Claudius reveals that although he has prayed, "Words without thoughts never to heaven go"; Hamlet could have damned Claudius, had the prince only carried out his impulse.

Hamlet himself suggests another of the popular theories: his "native hue of resolution / Is sicklied o'er with the pale cast of thought." In other words, he is not able to carry out the deeds which he has resolved to do, mired in his own "analysis paralysis." In Act II, Scene 2, Hamlet suggests that Denmark is a prison, and compares it to his mind: " . . . there is nothing either good or bad but thinking makes it so." This passage also supports the theory of action arrested by intellect.

The question of Hamlet's inaction is further complicated by the attitudes evidenced by several characters. The Player King tells the Player Queen that when her passions (i.e., her grief and loyalty) have cooled, her actions will be governed by other concerns and she will remarry. Hamlet chides Gertrude about her hasty remarriage, saying because of her age, she cannot have been ruled by her passions (i.e., lust), and must have been ruled by "judgment" (i.e., reason). The Ghost restrains Hamlet's rebuke of Gertrude, urging him to channel his anger at Claudius; in other words, to control his passions as he seeks vengeance. And when Hamlet pays tribute to his loyal friend Horatio, he remarks that Horatio is not "passion's slave," and whose "blood [passion] and judgment" is so well blended that he is not vulnerable to Fortune's "buffets and rewards." For Hamlet, the dilemma is the proper yoking of passion, which would spur him to immediate vengeance, with rea-

son, which is God-given, and which would temper Hamlet's actions with prudent judgment. Hamlet seems unable to strike the
balance, and is forever trying to weigh the emotional against the
rational. The result is his inaction.

Hamlet has been dubbed the Melancholy Dane because of the
many expressions of his sense of loss and grief at his father's death.
Elizabethans were familiar with the concept of *melancholia*, believed to be caused by an excess of the humour (bodily fluid), black
bile. The sufferer's moods would swing from deep depression and
self-deprecation, to highly emotional outbursts. Certainly Hamlet's
puzzling behavior, which appears insane to others, could be a
manifestation of this supposed disorder.

More modern critics note the Oedipal pattern in Hamlet's relationship with his mother. To the extent that Claudius has done
that which Hamlet himself desired to do (kill his father and marry
his mother), the personae of Claudius and Hamlet merge. To
avenge the murder-marriage is to commit suicide; indeed, Hamlet contemplates that very thing in his famous "To be or not to be"
speech. Perhaps Hamlet hesitates to kill Claudius because of religious strictures against suicide, rather than against murder.

Other critics believe that Hamlet fears the apparition of his
father is not an "honest Ghost," and that his uncertainty restrains
his vengeance. If the Ghost is "a devil . . . [in] a pleasing shape" who
"abuses [Hamlet] to damn [him]," then to take matters into his own
hands would go against Hamlet's religious beliefs. Beliefs of the
time held that royalty ruled by divine right, so the murder of
Hamlet's father would therefore call for divine justice. If Hamlet is
merely God's tool, the murder is divinely ordained and sanctioned.
However, if the Ghost is not heaven sent, if Hamlet seeks revenge
for his own purposes, the murder is not holy and Hamlet's revenge
against Claudius would be a sin. As he says, "I'll have grounds /
More relative than this;" he will let Claudius' reaction to the
"mousetrap" guide him, rather than depending solely on the
Ghost's injunction.

A very generous critical reading credits Hamlet with an aware-
ness of his own selfish motives; murdering Claudius would clear
the path to his own kingship. Hamlet suggests this thinking as he
explains his cause to Horatio, noting that Claudius "Popped in

between th' election and my hopes. . . . " He delays throughout the play, these critics say, because he wants to make sure that he is truly avenging his father, not merely seeking his own advancement.

Each of these major theories can be supported with textual evidence, some more strongly than others. Hamlet's obvious intellect and education might persuade the reader that he is less a victim of circumstances and more a creature tormented by his ability to see the situation from many angles, fraught with consequences political and spiritual, public and personal.

Hamlet's plan to have the players enact *The Murder of Gonzago* with the addition of "some dozen or sixteen lines which [he] would set down" is another example of the use of indirection to learn the truth. Of course, the players themselves embody this principle of "acting" or pretending, engaging in "seeming" rather than in "being." Hamlet alludes to this ironic duplicity when he notes the actor's ability to "drown the stage with [real] tears And cleave the general ear with horrid speech" over an imagined murder, while he himself, "the son of a dear father murdered," can only manage to curse his own inaction "like John-a-dreams."

If we think of the players as actors—those who do, who perform, who carry out resolve—Hamlet's invidious comparison of the player's performance to his own, further reinforces his disgust at his own delay and inaction in carrying out the Ghost's charge to avenge his father's death. For instance, at Ophelia's graveside, Hamlet insists that he loved her more than "forty thousand brothers," but later tells Horatio that "the bravery of [Laertes'] grief" made him forget himself, "For by the image of my cause I see / The portraiture of his."

Study Questions

1. What task does Polonius assign Reynaldo in Paris?

2. Why is Ophelia so upset when she speaks with her father?

3. In what respect does Polonius change his mind about Hamlet and the prince's relationship to Ophelia?

4. What task does Claudius assign to Rosencrantz and Guildenstern?

5. What news do Voltemand and Cornelius bring back from Norway?

6. What do Claudius and Gertrude conclude after hearing Polonius read the letter from Hamlet to Ophelia?

7. What does Polonius mean in an aside, as he speaks with Hamlet, "Though this be madness, yet there is method in't"?

8. What does Hamlet make Rosencrantz and Guildenstern confess?

9. Why have Hamlet's two friends arranged for the theatrical troupe to perform at the palace?

10. What is the significance of the speech which Hamlet requests from the actor, taken from the story of the Trojan War?

Answers

1. Polonius gives Reynaldo "money and . . . notes" to give to Laertes; and instructs him "to make [indirect] inquire / Of his behavior." Polonius wants to know what Laertes is doing in Paris, and intends "By indirections [to] find directions out."

2. "Affrighted," she reports that Hamlet came to her private room, his clothing undone and dirty, and his expression looking "As if he had been loosed out of hell / To speak of horrors—. . . . " He held her by the wrist and stared and sighed, and then went out the door, his eyes still on her "with his head over his shoulder turned."

3. Polonius diagnoses Hamlet's behavior as "the very ecstasy of love, / Whose violent property fordoes itself / And leads the will to desperate undertakings. . . . " He apologizes that he had earlier misjudged Hamlet, fearing "he did but trifle / And meant to wrack thee. . . . " He excuses his error by noting that it is as common for elders to be overcalculating as it is for youth to "lack discretion."

4. Claudius entreats the pair to remain at court for "Some little time" and "draw [Hamlet] on to pleasures" in an attempt to

learn what has caused his "transformation." Claudius says his motive is a desire to help Hamlet recover: " . . . Whether aught to us unknown afflicts him thus, That opened lies within our remedy."

5. Voltemand reports that the old King, uncle to young Fortinbras, had at first thought his nephew's preparations were for war against Poland. But, discovering they were "against your Highness," he stopped Fortinbras and rebuked him. Fortinbras promised never to wage war against Denmark, whereupon Norway rewarded his nephew with an annual allowance of "threescore thousand crowns" and sent him "against the Polack." Norway now asks for Fortinbras' "quiet pass Through [Claudius'] dominions for this enterprise. . . . "

6. Polonius states that since he instructed Ophelia to shun Hamlet, the prince's behavior has deteriorated from "a sadness, then into a fast, Thence to a watch, thence into a weakness, / Thence to a lightness, . . . Into the madness wherein now he raves. . . . " The Queen agrees: "It may be, very like." This is a shift from Gertrude's earlier assumption that "it is no other but the main, His father's death and our o'erhasty marriage."

7. Polonius realizes that although Hamlet's conversation with him seems irrational, it makes a certain kind of sense. The particular line reference has to do with the book which Hamlet purports to be reading, which is critical of old men and their infirmities and flaws. Hamlet points out that if Polonius "could go backward" like a crab, the old man would be the same age as Hamlet; therefore, Hamlet says, although he "most powerfully and potently" believes old men to be as the writer describes, he sees that he and Polonius are basically the same—that Polonius is just an older version of himself, or that he is just a younger version of Polonius. This reinforces what Polonius says: "'A is far gone, far gone. / And truly in my youth I suffered much extremity for love, very near this."

8. Hamlet urges them to reveal "whether you were sent for or no." After brief consultation, Guildenstern admits, "My lord, we were sent for." Hamlet then proceeds to explain why they have been sent for, detailing his own symptoms of depression and malaise.

9. Rosencrantz identifies the traveling company as "Even those you were wont to take such delight in, the tragedians of the city." The performance has been arranged for Hamlet's pleasure, apparently.

10. Hamlet praises the artistic quality of the play from which the scene is taken, noting that the play did not appeal to the masses. He asks particularly for " . . . Aeneas' tale to Dido, . . . especially when he speaks of Priam's slaughter." The allusion is to a play based on Virgil's *Aeneid*, the passage which tells how Pyrrhus, son of Achilles, extracts revenge upon the father (Priam) of Achilles' murderer (Paris). The intensity of the violence is horrifyingly graphic. This scene of revenge acts as a foil to Hamlet's own delay in avenging his father's murder.

Suggested Essay Topics

1. Draw a character profile of Polonius from his interactions in this act with Reynaldo (Scene 1), Ophelia (Scene 1), Gertrude and Claudius (Scene 2), Hamlet (Scene 2), and the Players (Scene 2).

2. Compare/contrast the relationship which the King and Queen have with Rosencrantz and Guildenstern, to the relationship which Hamlet has with Rosencrantz and Guildenstern, as defined in Scene 2.

Act III

Act III, Scene 1

Summary

In the presence of Polonius and Ophelia, King Claudius and Queen Gertrude question Rosencrantz and Guildenstern about their recent conversation with Hamlet; the pair report that although Hamlet confessed to being "distracted," he would not reveal the cause, evading questioning with "a crafty madness."

Hamlet's friends also report that Hamlet was pleased to learn of the visit of the traveling players, and that he has arranged a performance for that night, to which he has invited the King and Queen. The two men leave, and Claudius instructs Gertrude to leave also so as not to encounter Hamlet, for whom he has secretly sent, "That he, as 'twere by accident, may here / Affront Ophelia." Gertrude obeys, confiding to Ophelia her hope that Hamlet's love for Ophelia is the cause of his "wildness," and that her "virtues / Will bring him to his wonted way again. . . . " Claudius and Polonius instruct Ophelia to pretend to be reading a book of devotions so that Hamlet will find her solitude plausible. They depart just as Hamlet enters.

The Prince speaks to himself regarding the relative merits of life and death, "To be, or not to be." He weighs the troubles of living against the unknown nature of death and the afterlife. He compares death to sleep, sleep which is full of dreams which "must give us pause." When he notices Ophelia at her devotions, he asks her to pray for his sins. She tells Hamlet that she wishes to return some "remembrances" of his, but he denies that he gave her anything. She protests that he did give them, along with "words of sweet breath," which he also denies.

Hamlet then urges Ophelia to "Get thee to a nunnery," that all men are "arrant knaves," not to be believed. He then decries marriage in general, and says that "Those that are married already— all but one—shall live. The rest shall keep as they are." He exits, leaving Ophelia to lament his apparent insanity.

Polonius and Claudius emerge from their concealment. Claudius notes that Hamlet's words did not sound either like love or like madness, and announces that he will send Hamlet to England to collect overdue tribute. He hopes the change of scenery and the ocean voyage will get rid of the "something in his soul" which is bothering Hamlet. Polonius agrees to the King's plan, but urges one more attempt to discover the cause of Hamlet's "grief." after the play, Gertrude is to sound him out, and Polonius plans to eavesdrop. If this plan does not work, Polonius tells Claudius to send Hamlet to England, "or confine him where / Your wisdom best shall think." Claudius agrees, and says the "Madness in great ones must not unwatched go." They exit.

Analysis

This act begins with a stage crowded with those characters most closely associated with Hamlet, with the exception of Horatio and Laertes: Claudius, Gertrude, Polonius, Ophelia, Rosencrantz and Guildenstern. As each one is assigned his task in the discovery of Hamlet's malaise, that character departs. When at last the stage is empty but for Ophelia, Hamlet enters.

Every character is involved in duplicity at this point: Rosencrantz and Guildenstern are not being completely honest with Claudius, as they were not completely honest with Hamlet; Gertrude disappears so Hamlet does not suspect that he is being set up; Claudius and Polonius conceal themselves so they can eavesdrop; and Ophelia pretends to be in maidenly devotions in order to engage Hamlet in conversation.

Hamlet, meantime, has conceived of the Mousetrap in order to trick Claudius into exposing his guilt. The Prince then proceeds to lie to Ophelia, denying that he gave her "remembrances" or that

he spoke lovingly to her; she is convinced he is insane. At Polonius'
suggestion, Claudius continues his deceit with the plot to ship
Hamlet to England with Rosencrantz and Guildenstern, supposedly to collect overdue tribute.

Even after overhearing Hamlet's interlude with Ophelia, Polonius urges one final attempt to discern the cause of Hamlet's mental state: the scene in Gertrude's closet which, ironically, causes his own death. Polonius is not only overbearing and pompous, self-important and self-righteous; he is bent on orchestrating every step of every dance. It is his job to give counsel to the King; but he insists on giving advice to everyone: his son, his daughter, Hamlet, the Queen, Reynaldo; he even admits to having played Julius Caesar in the university, "and was accounted a good actor"—presumably he would advise the Players, if called upon.

Hamlet's remarks to Ophelia about marriage are worth noting. He says that all men are "arrant knaves," which is certainly the case in Claudius' court, as we have seen. But he also decrees that everyone who is presently married shall live, but one; and the rest "shall keep as they are," presumably unwed. Remember that Claudius and Polonius are eavesdropping; Claudius hears this "all but one." Surely he senses Hamlet's intent, for a few moments later, Claudius announces his plan to send Hamlet to England. As Claudius later reveals to the pair, this move is more for his own protection than for Hamlet's well-being.

Once again Polonius lays his heavy hand on the details, urging the King to either send Hamlet to England "or confine him where / Your wisdom best shall think." Polonius seems unconcerned whether Hamlet is a threat to his daughter's virtue or to Claudius' reign; Polonius sees an opportunity to exercise control and influence, and takes it—again and again.

Act III, Scene 2

Summary

Hamlet enters, giving instructions to several of the Players on the appropriate and most effective delivery of the "speech" which he has prepared for insertion into the evening's performance. As the Players exit, Polonius enters with Rosencrantz and Guildenstern, who inform Hamlet that Claudius and Gertrude have agreed to attend the play. Hamlet urges the trio to go help hasten the Players, then summons Horatio. Hamlet expresses his love and respect

for Horatio, then asks Horatio to scrutinize Claudius during the one scene which "comes near the circumstance . . . of my father's death." Horatio agrees.

Gertrude invites her son to sit beside her, but he refuses in favor of a seat with Ophelia, whom he engages in risque banter. The dumb show (pantomime) begins, enacting the murder of a King by one who pours poison in his ears; the widowed Queen at first appears disconsolate, but eventually accepts the love of the man who murdered her husband. Hamlet assures Ophelia that the actors will explain the meaning of the dumb show.

Following a brief Prologue, the Player King and Player Queen speak of love, death, and remarriage. The Player King and Queen discuss the likelihood of her remarriage after his impending death; she vows she will not, but he argues that when we make decisions in the heat of the moment, we fail to carry them out when the emotion fades: "What to ourselves in passion we propose, The passion ending, doth the purpose lose." The Player King also notes that fortune does not follow our desires; so "'tis not strange That even our loves should with our fortunes change."

The Player Queen declares that she would rather starve, be imprisoned, be without trust, hope, and joy, and have "lasting strife, If, once a widow, ever I be wife!", especially if the second husband had murdered the first. She says such a marriage would be for reasons of "thrift, but none of love," but the Player King argues that "So think thou wilt no second husband wed, / But die thy thoughts when thy first lord is dead."

When Claudius asks if this play is meant to give offense, Hamlet assures him "they do but jest, poison in jest; no offense i' th' world . . . we that have free souls, it touches us not." But as the play progresses and the actor portraying Lucianus (the king's nephew) pours poison in the sleeping king's ear, Hamlet comments, "You shall see anon how the murderer gets the love of Gonzago's wife." Claudius bolts from his seat, Polonius ends the performance and calls for lights, and everyone leaves except Hamlet and Horatio. They believe they have exposed Claudius, proving the Ghost's validity.

Rosencrantz and Guildenstern enter, and urge Hamlet to obey his mother's request that he come to her before he goes to bed. The pair attempt to persuade Hamlet to reveal the "cause of distemper," but he evades their questions and accuses them of trying to play upon him like the recorders the Players have just entered with: "Call me what instrument you will, though you can fret me, you cannot play upon me." Polonius enters and repeats Gertrude's request, which Hamlet says he will heed. When all others have departed, Hamlet resolves to hold his anger in check, rebuking his mother but not harming her.

Analysis

The second scene also opens with a full stage as Hamlet addresses the Players about dramatic delivery; as the Players depart to make ready, Polonius enters with Rosencrantz and Guildenstern. Hamlet quickly moves that trio offstage to "hasten" the Players. Then Horatio enters, and he and Hamlet speak as dear and close friends. Horatio, who had earlier been enlisted by Claudius and Gertrude to sound out Hamlet, now sides with his long time friend and school mate—more duplicity.

This technique repeated from Scene 1, of many becoming few, stresses the increasing intensity of the machinations of the opposing forces: Claudius' in the first, and Hamlet's in the second. They mirror each other, but are inverse images: evil for good. But now the stage again fills to overflowing with the Players, the members of the royal court, the lords and ladies attendant thereon, and Guards with torches. Hamlet refuses his mother's invitation to sit beside her, going instead to Ophelia and engaging in bawdy innuendoes.

Shakespeare has crowded the stage and placed Ophelia and Hamlet front and center with seemingly inappropriate and confusing dialogue. When Hamlet comments that his mother has remarried not "*two hours*" after his father's death, Ophelia remarks that it is "*twice two months.*" But when he restates the matter, he makes it only "*two months.*" Likewise, the Players were originally scheduled to perform "tomorrow night;" but moments later, they are hurrying to make ready for the performance "presently" that very night. This seeming confusion over chronology is really Shakespeare's way of telescoping time, lending urgency to the matter at hand—Hamlet's revenge on the murderer of his father.

As the dumb show concludes, Ophelia asks Hamlet what it means; he answers "mischief," referring to his plan to expose Claudius. The Prologue does not satisfy Ophelia's curiosity, and she notes that "'Tis brief, my lord." Hamlet answers, "As woman's love," returning to his theme of his mother's infidelity to her dead husband's memory. Hamlet, pursuing his "mischief," asks his mother, "how like you this play?" Gertrude answers, "The lady doth protest too much, methinks," suggesting that from her perspective, remarriage would not be an impossibility for a widow. Hamlet replies, "O, but she'll keep her word," implying that the Player Queen, at least, is faithful to her vows—an invidious comparison that surely is not lost on Gertrude.

Guildenstern and Rosencrantz, sent to summon Hamlet to his mother's room, reveal that Claudius is "in . . . marvelous [distemper]," not from drink, as Hamlet suggests, but from "choler" (anger). Hamlet's suggestion that they should rather be summoning a doctor to purge the king and make him well is a foreshadowing of the imagery he will use when he finds Claudius at prayer: "This physic but prolongs thy sickly days." When Rosencrantz and Guildenstern report back to Claudius a few moments later, they speak of the necessity of protecting the king's health against any harm that may be intended by Hamlet. Their remarks make clear that the life of "majesty," upon whom so many other lives depend, is of far greater importance than an ordinary man's life.

This conversation helps to justify Hamlet's later action of sealing their death warrant; they have tried to "play upon [him]", taking Claudius' part against him. Hamlet explains to Horatio that he does not feel guilty for their fates; the pair simply got caught between the thrustings "of mighty opposites." His pragmatic view ironically echoes their own attitude, that the life of the king is more important than any other's; since Hamlet had hoped to become king (by election) at his father's death, he is the "majesty" this time around, not Claudius.

Act III, Scene 3

Summary

Claudius enters with Rosencrantz and Guildenstern; Claudius is convinced that Hamlet, in his "madness," means to harm him in some way. He proposes to send Hamlet to England, along with Rosencrantz and Guildenstern, for safety's sake. They agree, noting that the fortunes of "Majesty" always affect the lives of many others besides itself. This voyage is to commence at once.

Polonius enters to inform Claudius that Hamlet is on his way to Gertrude's private room; Polonius announces that he will hide "behind the arras," in order to "o'erhear" their conversation. Polonius says he expects Gertrude to severely scold Hamlet, but notes that, as Hamlet's mother, she will be biased toward anything he may say to her. Thus, "'Tis meet that some more audience than a mother" should hear Hamlet's remarks. Polonius promises Claudius that he will return with a full report before the king goes to bed.

Claudius then soliloquizes about his guilt over the murder of his own brother, which he compares to the murder of Abel by Cain. Claudius laments the fact that he is unable to pray and thus receive mercy, which would cleanse him of this sin. He suspects that his offense would not be forgiven, since he retains all the benefits

deriving from the murder: "My crown, mine own ambition, and my queen." Perhaps on earth one can "[Buy] out the law. But 'tis not so above." At last, the king manages to kneel in a final attempt at repentance.

Hamlet enters, sees Claudius apparently at prayer, and reasons that to murder Claudius now would "send [this same villain] To heaven" rather than to hell. He vows to wait and kill Claudius—as Claudius had killed Hamlet's father—"full of bread, / With all his crimes broad blown, as flush as May," while the king is "about some act / That has no relish of salvation in't—. . . . " Hamlet notes that Claudius' prayer has only postponed his eventual death.

Ironically, as Hamlet exits, Claudius rises, and discloses that he has still been unable to pray and receive the spiritual peace he seeks: "My words fly up, my thoughts remain below. Words without thoughts never to heaven go."

Analysis

Prominently foregrounded in this scene is Claudius' guilt and the fear which attends it. He imagines—rightly so—that Hamlet means to harm him. And he feels the need to repent before heaven in order to escape eternal damnation. Thus Claudius fears both earthly and divine retribution, and in this scene both are postponed. Hamlet waits until a more suitable time to kill the king, and Claudius finds himself unable to pray with satisfactory results.

The importance given to Claudius' life, as "majesty," is ironic; for Claudius has murdered his brother—also "majesty"—and Hamlet, likely to be elected "majesty," is on Claudius' trail. The question of whose life is most important in the grand scheme of things is therefore moot, since the former King, Claudius, and Hamlet all have a claim to that coveted seat.

Act III, Scene 4

Summary

Polonius urges the Queen to be sharply critical of Hamlet's actions, and to tell him that she has had to intercede on his behalf, standing "between / Much heat and him." Polonius then hides be-

hind the wall tapestry as Hamlet enters. Hamlet speaks very directly to his mother, telling her that she has offended his father, and proposes revealing her "innermost part" to her. Gertrude cries out in fear that Hamlet means to murder her, prompting Polonius to call out from behind the curtain. Hamlet, supposing the eaves-dropper to be Claudius, thrusts his sword through the curtain, killing Polonius, over whom Hamlet says, "Thou wretched, rash, intruding fool, farewell! I took thee for thy better." Hamlet scolds the old man for being "too busy," thus endangering his own life. Hamlet then insists that his mother sit down and hear him out; she continues to berate him for his rudeness and claims not to know what act or deed of hers he speaks of "that roars so loud and thunders. . . ."

Hamlet produces two images, one of his father, the other of his uncle. He contrasts them for Gertrude, expressing his disbelief that she could have so soon forgotten her first husband, on whom "every god did seem to set his seal / To give the world assurance of a man." He reasons that she cannot have been driven by passion, "for at [her] age / The heyday in the blood is tame, . . . And waits upon the judgment, and what judgment / Would step from this to this?" He finally declares that virtue melts and all shame disappears when passion rules over reason.

Gertrude begs Hamlet to stop, for she now sees her guilt; but he continues to recount her sin of incest with "A murderer and a villain, / A slave that is not twentieth part the tithe / Of your precedent lord, a vice of kings, / A cutpurse of the empire and the rule, . . . " Then the Ghost enters, visible only to Hamlet, who asks if his father has come to scold him for not yet carrying out his revenge. The Ghost directs Hamlet to comfort his mother, who is very disturbed by Hamlet's words and by his speaking to "th' incorporal air."

Gertrude is certain that Hamlet is mad, but he urges her to realize that it is not his madness but "[her] trespass" that speaks. He begs her to "Confess [herself] to heaven, / Repent what's past, avoid what is to come. . . . " He asks her to refrain from sleeping with Claudius that night, "And that shall lend a kind of easiness /

To the next abstinence. . . . " Further, Hamlet tells her not to reveal to Claudius that he is not really mad, and she agrees. He reminds her that he is scheduled to sail to England with Rosencrantz and Guildenstern, whom he does not trust anymore than "adders fanged." But he tells his mother that he plans to outsmart them. Hamlet then drags Polonius out of the room, calling his body "the guts." He notes that while alive, Polonius was "a foolish, prating knave," but that he is now "most still, most secret, and most grave. . . . "

Analysis

Hamlet continues with imagery of health and disease in his conversation with Gertrude. He insists that he is healthy, not mad. He pleads with her to recognize that her "trespass" "will but skin and film the ulcerous place Whiles rank corruption, [under]mining all within, Infects unseen." This image also echoes the play's persistent motif of appearance vs. reality, seeming vs. being, deception vs. honesty.

Study Questions

1. What do Rosencrantz and Guildenstern report to Claudius regarding their conversation with Hamlet?

2. What do the pair fail to reveal to Claudius?

3. What favor does Hamlet ask of Horatio?

4. What is the plot of the Dumb Show the Players present?

5. What is the significance of the play's title, "The Mousetrap"?

6. What does Hamlet mean, as he prepares to visit his mother, when he says, "O heart, lose not thy nature"?

7. What rationale do Rosencrantz and Guildenstern give for accepting Claudius' commission to take Hamlet to England forthwith?

8. What is ironic about Hamlet's failure to kill Claudius while the King is kneeling in prayer?

9. What is Hamlet's reaction when he realizes he has killed

Polonius rather than Claudius, whom he had presumed to be the one hiding behind the curtain?

10. What is the apparent purpose of the Ghost's appearance in the Queen's bedroom while Hamlet speaks with his mother?

Answers

1. They say Hamlet was polite but not very inclined to talk about what was bothering him. They report that Hamlet seemed pleased that the Players had been engaged for a performance.

2. They do not disclose that Hamlet made them admit that they had been sent by Claudius, nor that Hamlet revealed that Claudius and Gertrude are deceived about his seeming madness.

3. He wants Horatio to carefully observe Claudius during the play, to watch his reactions, to help to determine whether the Ghost which named Claudius murderer was heaven sent or from "Vulcan's stithy."

4. A queen and king make affectionate show; he lies down and falls asleep, she leaves. Another man enters and pours poison in the king's ear, and leaves. The queen returns, is distraught, but is eventually comforted and ultimately seduced by the poisoner himself.

5. The play "is the image of a murder done in Vienna," and is, in fact, entitled, "The Murder of Gonzago," which Hamlet specifically requests the Players to perform with the addition of the lines which he inserts. That he tells Claudius it is called, "The Mousetrap," suggests his ulterior motive, especially since he continues, "Your Majesty, and we that have free souls, it touches us not." The clear implication is that Claudius does not have a clear conscience, and will, therefore, be "touched" by the play—as he obviously is.

6. He does not wish to forget that she is his mother, whom he does not mean to harm; on the other hand, he wants to re-

buke her for her actions. He remarks on this inconsistency:
"My tongue and soul in this be hypocrites."

7. They say that because so many lives depend upon a king's
life, he must be protected. A king's death acts like a "gulf"
(whirlpool) and sucks whoever is nearby down with it. Whatever affects the king, affects the populace as a whole: "Never
alone Did the King sigh, but with a general groan."

8. Claudius kneels but is unable to pray. Had Hamlet killed him
then, as he first intended, Claudius' soul would have been
damned.

9. Hamlet is disrespectful to Polonius, and not in the least remorseful about his error. In essence he says Polonius was a
busy body who deserved what he got. He "[lugs] the guts"
into the next room without respect or ceremony. He does
say that he repents Polonius' death, but says he was only
acting as heaven's "scourge and minister," and knows that
he "will answer well / The death [he] gave him."

10. The Ghost says, "This visitation Is but to whet thy almost
blunted purpose." Hamlet has been carried away in scolding his mother for her marriage to his father's brother, a man
much inferior to her husband. Gertrude has repeatedly cried
for Hamlet to "speak no more," but he has been unrelenting. The Ghost now reminds Hamlet of his task of revenge,
and bids him give comfort now to his mother, on whom
"amazement . . . sits." Because she can neither hear nor see
the Ghost, she concludes that Hamlet is truly insane; the
Ghost asks Hamlet to "step between her and her fighting
soul!"

Suggested Essay Topics

1. Discuss the thematic connection between Hamlet's scene
with Ophelia where he speaks of *honesty*, his speech to the
Players on *acting*, and his speech to Horatio on *flattery*.

2. Compare Claudius' thoughts on his own guilt as he tries to
pray to Gertrude's recognition of her guilt when confronted
by Hamlet.

3. Discuss the grouping of characters from scene to scene in
    Act III, beginning with a crowded stage in Scene 1 and end-
    ing with Gertrude alone in Scene 4. What does Shakespeare
    achieve with the rapidly changing cast on stage as the ac-
    tion in this act unfolds?

Act IV

Act IV, Scene 1

Summary

Claudius, Gertrude, Rosencrantz and Guildenstern enter; Claudius remarks on Gertrude's sighing, which he asks her to explain. She dismisses the two young men, and then relates to Claudius the recent events in her closet; she says Hamlet, "in his lawless fit," has killed Polonius. Claudius notes that he himself would have been killed, had he been the one hiding behind the curtain. He regrets that, out of love for Hamlet, he neglected to do what was best; that is, he "Should have kept short, restrained, and out of haunt / This mad young man," but instead "let [him] feed / Even on the pith of life" like a disease kept unacknowledged.

Gertrude reveals that Hamlet, who has gone to remove Polonius' body, "weeps for what is done," which she says proves his madness is genuine. Claudius reminds Gertrude that he is shipping Hamlet out at daybreak, which must be made acceptable to the court. He summons Rosencrantz and Guildenstern and bids them hasten to find Hamlet, "speak fair," and bring Polonius' body into the chapel. They leave, and Claudius advises Gertrude that they must tell their "wisest friends" what has happened to Polonius, and that they are sending Hamlet away. The King hopes, by coupling these two events, to throw all ill will toward Hamlet, avoiding any taint of slander himself. They exit, with Claudius "full of discord and dismay."

Analysis

Act IV begins with four relatively short scenes, presenting the King and Queen; then Hamlet with Rosencrantz and Guildenstern; then Rosencrantz, Guildenstern, Hamlet, and the King; then Hamlet, Rosencrantz and Guildenstern with the Captain of Fortinbras' army. Shakespeare is speeding up the action in these brief scenes, quickening the pace as Claudius moves swiftly to protect himself from Hamlet, even as Hamlet baits him by playing hide-and-seek with Polonius' body. When Hamlet and the others encounter Fortinbras, Hamlet desires to get on with his appointed task of avenging his father. Shakespeare thus continues the sense of building urgency in this act.

Act IV, Scene 2

Summary

Hamlet enters, having "Safely stowed" the body of Polonius. Rosencrantz and Guildenstern enter, seeking the corpse, but Hamlet won't tell where it is hidden, saying only he has "Compounded it with dust, whereto 'tis kin." Then Hamlet calls Rosencrantz a "sponge . . . that soaks up the King's countenance, his rewards, his authorities." But that when the King needs what they "have gleaned, it is but squeezing you and, sponge, you shall be dry again." When they ask again of the body's whereabouts, Hamlet again refuses to say, but agrees to go with them to the King, whom Hamlet says is "a thing . . . Of nothing." Hamlet dashes offstage as if they are pursuing him in a game of hide-and-seek: "Hide fox, and all after."

Analysis

True to her word to Hamlet, Gertrude is at great pains to assure Claudius that Hamlet's madness is genuine. She even stretches the truth by saying Hamlet "weeps for what is done"—Hamlet repents, but says "heaven hath pleased it so, . . . That I must be their scourge and minister." Claudius is at equally great pains to convince Gertrude that he is acting in Hamlet's best interest in shipping him off to England. Claudius plans to manipulate the public disclosure of information to his best advantage. Similarly he will attempt to manipulate England's allegiance in arranging Hamlet's murder (Scene 3), and to manipulate Laertes' anger by excusing his own inaction out of love for Gertrude and public sentiment for Hamlet (Scene 7).

Act IV, Scene 3

Summary

Claudius enters with several men, whom he has told of Hamlet's murder of Polonius, and that he has "sent to seek him and to find the body." He tells them it is dangerous to allow Hamlet to remain at large, but that because of Hamlet's popularity among the "distracted multitude," his punishment must not seem too heavy; the public only judge what they can see, and weigh only the punishment, "But never the offense." Claudius says Hamlet's sudden leaving must seem to be part of a careful plan in order to keep things "all smooth and even."

Rosencrantz and Guildenstern enter and report that Hamlet will not reveal the location of Polonius' body, and that Hamlet is waiting outside. Claudius summons him, but Hamlet will only tell the King, first, that Polonius is "At supper," where he is being eaten by worms; and second, that Polonius is in heaven, or perhaps in hell. But finally he reveals that Polonius can be found "as you go up the stairs into the lobby" where he "will stay till you come."

The King tells Hamlet that, for his own safety, he is being sent to England at once. Hamlet then bids the King farewell, calling him "dear Mother," since "father and mother is man and wife, man and wife is one flesh, and so, my mother." Hamlet exits, and Claudius orders the others to follow him and get him on board ship without delay, since everything that depends on this aspect of his plan is all "sealed and done."

Left alone, Claudius expresses his hope that England will obey the letters that Rosencrantz and Guildenstern carry which call for Hamlet's "present death." He notes that England is still in awe of Denmark because of past defeats, and he hopes that this fear will insure their cooperation. He says that Hamlet is like a fever in his blood which must be cured, or Claudius can not have happiness, no matter what else may befall him.

Analysis

Although Claudius is trying desperately to orchestrate the events to Hamlet's disadvantage, Hamlet remains in control despite his seeming madness. All Claudius and the others can do is react to Hamlet's inane remarks and puzzling actions. Claudius is struggling both at home and abroad—in England—to rally public opinion and political power into his own camp.

Act IV, Scene 4

New Characters:

Young Fortinbras: *nephew to the aged king of Norway*

Captain: *officer in Fortinbras' army*

Summary

Fortinbras sends his Captain to Claudius, seeking escort for his army's safe march through Denmark. He says if the King wishes, he will meet personally with him. Fortinbras exits with his army. Hamlet and Rosencrantz enter and learn from the Captain that the army, headed for "some part of Poland," means to attack a "little patch of ground that hath in it no profit but the name," not worth "five ducats." Hamlet doubts the Poles will defend such a worthless area, but the Captain tells him "it is already garrisoned." Hamlet comments that "Two thousand souls and twenty thousand ducats" is a high price to pay for something so worthless, and notes that this sort of behavior results from "much wealth and peace," destroying from within like an abscess.

Left alone, having sent his companions on ahead, Hamlet notes that events are conspiring to spur his revenge. He says a man who only eats and sleeps is but a beast; surely God gave us *reason*. He wonders why he does not act on his thoughts, since he has "cause, and will, and strength, and means To do't." Hamlet says that even young Fortinbras, "a delicate and tender prince," takes great risk for little gain, "When honor's at the stake." Hamlet notes his own great motivations ("a father killed, a mother stained") do not move him to action, while Fortinbras' army is about to engage in a battle in which more men will be killed than the worthless land they fight for can hold in burial. He vows to have only "bloody" thoughts from now on.

Analysis

In Scene 4, Hamlet is moved to note his own delay and inaction in seeking revenge, as contrasted with the willingness of Fortinbras' and the Polish armies to fight and die for nothing more than honor. Their battlefield is nearly worthless, but he has great motive: "a father killed, a mother stained."

Act IV, Scene 5

Summary

Horatio, Gertrude, and a Gentleman enter. At Horatio's urging, the Queen finally agrees to speak with Ophelia, who the Gentleman reports to be in a distracted, pitiable state, babbling nonsense about her dead father. Ophelia enters singing of a dead man, and a maid deflowered. Claudius enters, and seeing her state, orders Horatio to "Follow her close; give her good watch." Alone with Gertrude, Claudius relays all the bad news from court: Polonius' murder and hasty burial, Hamlet's "remove" to England, public unrest at Polonius' death, Ophelia's madness, and Laertes' secret return from France and his suspicions that Claudius is somehow responsible for Polonius' death. Claudius says all these events are killing him, like shrapnel from a cannon, "in many places."

A Messenger enters with news that Laertes has overtaken the King's officers, and is now being hailed as the "rabble's" choice for king. Gertrude laments that the "false Danish dogs" are on the wrong trail. Laertes bursts in upon the King and Queen, insists that those accompanying him wait outside, and angrily demands to know the whereabouts of his father. Gertrude attempts to restrain Laertes from accusing or harming Claudius, but Claudius declares that, as King, he is divinely protected from treason, and humors

Laertes' wrath. Claudius assures Laertes that he had nothing to do with Polonius' death, and that he grieves deeply for his demise.

Ophelia enters, singing of her father's death and distributing imaginary flowers, apparently quite mad and unresponsive to Laertes' comments to her. Laertes is touched by her state and moved to revenge. When Ophelia leaves, Claudius implores Laertes to hear him out in the presence of whichever of Laertes' friends the young man would select, "to judge 'twixt you and me." Claudius vows to relinquish everything, including his life, to Laertes if he is found responsible for Polonius' death. They depart to discuss Polonius' "means of death" and his improper, unceremonious burial.

Analysis

Scene 5 presents yet another contrast to Hamlet's delay; Laertes bursts in upon the King and Queen and demands to know about his father's death. Gertrude, in her accustomed role as peacemaker and restrainer-of-violent-men, tries to soothe Laertes' wrath over his father's death and his sister's madness; and Claudius, in his usual self-serving half-truth declaration, swears to forfeit everything if he is directly or indirectly responsible for Polonius' death. That the "rabble" have proclaimed Laertes their choice for King makes it doubly important that Claudius keep Laertes from harboring any animosity toward him. To have murdered the king, only to be impeached by the fickle populace, would make Claudius' sins weigh heavily indeed.

Ophelia presents perhaps the furthest end of a spectrum on which sit also Hamlet, Laertes, and young Fortinbras. In the face of her father's death, she goes crazy. Perhaps Shakespeare makes a gender distinction here, as Laertes (Scene 7) forbids his tears on hearing of Ophelia's death, but says when he is alone, "The woman will be out." Woman, as weaker or gentler, cannot bear the heavy burden as well as man; Ophelia loses that capacity (reason) which Hamlet notes several times in the play is what separates us from beasts. Hamlet's madness is, while convincing to many who witness it, completely feigned. He is admittedly tormented by his conflicting desires and fears, but he is not crazy. He needs constant prompting in his vengeance, and continually berates himself for his weak resolve.

On the other hand, Laertes acts promptly at the news of his slain father, seeking the villain even in the King's chambers; but he is easily turned aside and manipulated by Claudius, who turns him into a tool against Hamlet—Laertes' friend and Claudius' enemy. And Fortinbras, after a false start to attack Denmark, whose former king slew his father, is redirected against Poland in a battle over land not worth dying for, purely for principle and honor. Not one of these children really achieves a satisfactory resolution in the search for vengeance.

Act IV, Scene 6

New Characters:

Sailors: *seafaring men who bring news from Hamlet*

Summary

Horatio and a few others are accosted by Sailors with a letter from Hamlet to Horatio, detailing his capture at sea by pirates, who, he says, treated him well. The letter instructs Horatio to deliver the "letters I have sent" to the King, and then come at once to him, guided by "these good fellows." Hamlet adds that Rosencrantz and Guildenstern still sail toward England, and says "Of them I have much to tell thee."

Horatio promises to reward the Sailors for delivering the messages.

Analysis

The unlikely capture-rescue of Hamlet by the pirates is, of course, dramatically necessary to effect Hamlet's return to Denmark, but it strains plausibility even more than the turn of events in the final sword fight (Act V, Scene 2). The interface between possibility and plausibility is stretched taut. This unlikely series of events, however, does reinforce Hamlet's frequent remarks about the role of fate in men's lives.

Hamlet's use of the phrase, "compelled valor," echoes his rebuke to his mother in Act III, Scene 4: "Assume a virtue, if you have it not." As Hamlet feigned bravery in boarding the pirate ship, Gertrude was urged to feign virtue in absenting herself from Claudius' bed. The motif of illusion versus reality, seeming versus being, play acting versus genuine, is again foregrounded.

Act IV, Scene 7

Summary

Laertes asks Claudius why, as King, he did not act against Hamlet, whom Claudius accuses of "[pursuing] my life." Claudius cites two reasons. First, his own love for Gertrude, whose love for Hamlet is so great that he cannot counteract it. Second, the love the general public has for Hamlet makes it impossible for them to see Hamlet's faults; they would tend to turn Claudius' accusations back upon himself. Claudius tries to assure Laertes that they are united in their love of Polonius and in their desire for revenge against Hamlet for his plottings.

A Messenger enters with letters from Hamlet, for Claudius and for Gertrude. Hamlet tells the King that he has landed "naked [without any means or provisions] on your kingdom," and asks to see Claudius the next day, at which time he will "recount the occasion of my sudden and more strange return." The postscript adds, "alone." Claudius enlists Laertes in a plot to kill Hamlet which is so foolproof that even Gertrude will "call it accident." The King flatters Laertes' skills as a fencer, and says Hamlet is so envious of Laertes' reputation that he will accept a challenge to duel Laertes, especially if he believes that Claudius has wagered on the outcome.

Laertes vows to poison his sword tip to insure Hamlet's death if he be "but scratched withal." As double insurance, Claudius promises to poison a drink, which Hamlet will call for "When in your motion you are hot and dry" toward the end of the bout.

Gertrude enters with news that Ophelia has drowned in the stream as she tried to hang flower garlands on the willow branches. Laertes withholds his tears as too womanly, and leaves in an agitated state. Claudius tells Gertrude that he had to work hard to calm Laertes, and now fears that "this will give it start again," so they follow Laertes.

Analysis

Claudius is again—or still—struggling to maintain control of the situation, but now it is Laertes who threatens to upset the King's plans. Claudius puts on a show of bravado in the face of Laertes' demands, and insinuates Laertes into his plot against Hamlet. Now Claudius openly intends to deceive Gertrude as he murders her son; previously he had deceived her covertly in the murder of her husband. That Claudius is ruthless as well as resolute becomes apparent when, at news of Ophelia's death, the King says they need to watch Laertes to keep him calm. His true motive, of course, is to protect his own position against Laertes, whom the people have proclaimed as their choice for king.

Study Questions

1. What is Claudius' response when Gertrude tells him that Hamlet has murdered Polonius?

2. What does Claudius direct Rosencrantz and Guildenstern to do?

3. Why does Hamlet hide Polonius' corpse and then dash away when Rosencrantz and Guildenstern question him about it?

4. Why does Hamlet call Claudius "dear Mother"?

5. Why does Fortinbras send word to the Danish king (Claudius)?

6. How does Hamlet contrast himself (all men) to beasts?

7. How does Claudius propose to satisfy Laertes' suspicions?

8. What reasons does Claudius give Laertes for not taking action against Hamlet, who, Claudius says, "Pursued [his] life"?

9. Why does Claudius plan to poison the drink, in addition to poisoning the rapier tip which Laertes will wield?

10. How does Ophelia drown?

Answers

1. He says he himself would have been killed, had he been behind the curtain; that Hamlet's continued freedom threatens him, the Queen herself, and everyone. He fears he will be blamed for not keeping Hamlet restrained, but that love often prevents us from seeing the best course. Claudius tells her that Hamlet must be sent away (by ship), and that they must make people understand and approve their actions.

2. He directs them to get help and find Hamlet, "speak fair" to him, and bring Polonius' body into the chapel; "I pray you haste in this."

3. Hamlet is continuing in his "madness," behaving in ways which seem irrational to his family and friends. His seeming insanity will also act as a kind of shield for him; how can Claudius order his punishment for Polonius' murder if he was mad? Madmen are not responsible for their actions. Finally, Hamlet is taking delight in tormenting those who are obviously humoring him, while at the same time plotting against him.

4. Because "father and mother" equal "man and wife," and "man and wife" is one flesh, Claudius and Gertrude are one and the same. Hence, Claudius can be called "mother" and, presumably, Gertrude could be called "father."

5. He wants Claudius to provide safe escort for his (Norwegian) army as they march across Denmark, as Claudius had earlier promised.

6. He says a man who spends his time merely sleeping and feeding is only a beast; God gave man reason, to see both ahead and behind, not to become moldy from disuse. He can't decide if "thinking too precisely on th' event" is "bes-

tial oblivion [forgetfulness]" or "some craven scruple." He believes such thoughts are one part wisdom and three parts cowardice; since he has "cause, and will, and strength, and means to do't," he doesn't see why he hesitates.

7. He tells Laertes to gather his choice of his wisest friends to hear Claudius' version of the events; he promises to give up everything, including his life, if he be shown to have caused—directly or indirectly—Polonius' death. Otherwise, he asks Laertes to join with him to give Laertes' soul "content." Laertes specifies that he wants the answers to a number of issues surrounding his father's death, and Claudius agrees, adding, "where th' offense is, let the great ax fall."

8. Claudius says that Hamlet's mother "Lives almost by [Hamlet's] looks, and . . . She is so conjunctive to [Claudius'] life and soul," that the King cannot do anything which would hurt her. Secondly, he says that public sentiment is so solidly behind Hamlet that his sins would be transformed "to graces," and Claudius' charges would fall on himself rather than "where [he] had aimed them."

9. If the sword point does not work properly, and their true purpose be discovered, the tainted cup, offered to Hamlet when he is "hot and dry," will insure his death. Claudius, having bet on Hamlet to win, will be above suspicion in his death.

10. She is trying to hang flower garlands on the branches of a weeping willow which overhangs a brook; the branch breaks, spilling her into the water. Her clothes puff out and buoy her up for awhile, but eventually become saturated and pull her "to muddy death."

Suggested Essay Topics

1. Trace the way Claudius tries to manipulate the following characters in this act in order to achieve his own ends: Gertrude, Rosencrantz and Guildenstern, Hamlet, and Laertes.

2. Discuss the implications of Ophelia's song lyrics. What do
    they suggest about her relationship with Hamlet, and her
    grief for her father, especially as causes for her apparent
    madness?

SECTION SIX

Act V

Act V, Scene 1

New Characters:

Two Clowns: *rustics who are digging Ophelia's grave*

Doctor of Divinity: *priest who presides at Ophelia's burial*

Summary

The two rustics discuss the particulars of Ophelia's death and burial. The coroner has ruled that she shall have a Christian burial, which would mean that her death was accidental. But the men believe that Ophelia must have drowned herself, and suicide would prevent her from having a Christian burial. They decide that because she is a gentlewoman, she—like her class—is more privileged to drown or hang herself than are her fellow Christians. They make grisly jokes as they continue digging; then one sends the other to fetch him a tankard of beer. The one left digging sings about love and the brevity of life, as Hamlet and Horatio come upon him.

Horatio reasons that the man's exposure to these matters has hardened him to death. The Clown roughly throws out a number of skulls, to which Horatio and Hamlet assign identities such as politician, courtier, a Lord or Lady, lawyer, and buyer of land. When they inquire whose grave the Clown digs, he replies it is for a woman. The Clown reveals that he has been a gravedigger since Hamlet's father overcame old Fortinbras, the very day that young Hamlet was born. He answers Hamlet's further inquiries by noting

that young Hamlet was sent to England because he was mad, and
will return when he is better: "or, if 'a do not, 'tis no great matter
there . . . There the men are as mad as he." The Clown identifies
one skull as Yorick's, the King's jester, whom Hamlet says "hath
borne me on his back a thousand times." They continue discuss-

ing mortality and the return of man, no matter how noble, to the dust from whence he came.

From some distance, Horatio and Hamlet see the King, Queen, Laertes, a Doctor of Divinity, and various Lords entering with a coffin. The priest tells Laertes that because of her "doubtful" death, Ophelia cannot have complete rites, such as "To sing a requiem," and must lie "in ground unsanctified . . . Till the last trumpet." Gertrude strews flowers over the body, saying she had hoped "[Ophelia's] bride bed to have decked," not her grave. Laertes leaps

into the grave to hold his sister one last time before they cover her, and then asks that they bury him too.

At that, Hamlet comes forward to protest Laertes' actions: "I loved Ophelia. Forty thousand brothers / Could not with all their quantity of love / Make up my sum." The two men struggle, and are finally parted by Horatio and the attendants. Gertrude and Claudius assure Laertes that Hamlet's words and actions are "mere madness" which will soon pass. Horatio ushers Hamlet out, and Claudius urges Laertes to patiently await the working out of the plot of which they spoke earlier.

Analysis

Just as Act I began and ended with the appearance of the Ghost, Act V begins with the graveyard scene and ends with the multiple murders and imminent funeral rites. Throughout this final act are numerous references to death, as well as discussions of man's mortality. The rustics believe Ophelia, as a member of the gentility, to have special privilege in regard to her burial; but Hamlet and Horatio note that the unearthed skulls might belong to a person from any social class. Even Hamlet's once-beloved jester, Yorick, is sickening in his inevitable decomposition. That death and decay is the common end of all mankind underlies Hamlet's remarks to Horatio, where he notes that Alexander and Caesar could, in death, "stop a beer barrel" or "patch a wall."

This scene echoes Act IV in which Hamlet tells Claudius that Polonius is "At supper," meaning that he is now being eaten by maggots, and describes the food chain that enables "a king [to] go a progress through the guts of a beggar." Even the gravedigger sings of his youthful days of sweet love making, which have fallen victim to "age with his stealing steps," which "hath shipped me into the land, / As if I had never been such."

When the Clown reveals that he has been digging graves since the day of Hamlet's birth, the juxtaposition of death and birth cannot be ignored. Furthermore, the coincidence of the former King's victory over old Fortinbras on that same day lends a nobility to Hamlet by right of his royal birth. Yorick's skull, while part of the comic business, is another juxtaposition of youth (Hamlet's) with death (the jester's). This blending of the personal with the political is a motif upon which the revenge theme relies heavily throughout the play.

The hand of Fate is heavy, especially in this last act. Hamlet voices his belief that "There's a divinity that shapes our ends, Rough-hew them how we will." The series of coincidences which began with the accidental murder of Polonius in Act III continues with the incredibly easy exchange of death warrants for Guildenstern and Rosencrantz in place of his own, Hamlet's capture/rescue by the pirates, his unwillingness to postpone the fencing match with Laertes, his refusal of the poisoned cup until he finishes the bout, and the subsequent mistaken poisonings of Gertrude and Laertes. All of these events feed into the sense of inevitability and injustice, qualities which heighten the tragedy in this play, as they

do in classical tragedy. That Hamlet's own weaknesses compound
the external circumstances help define the play as Elizabethan, in
which the protagonist's flawed nature conspires to bring the uni-
verse down upon him.

Act V, Scene 2

Summary

Hamlet explains to Horatio how he managed to switch the letter which Rosencrantz and Guildenstern carried, ordering Hamlet's death, for one which ordered their own upon their arrival in England. Because of how smoothly this "changling" occurred, Hamlet expresses his belief that fate, or some "divinity," works out the details of our lives even when we have only a rough plan. Hamlet says that he feels no guilt for ordering the deaths of Rosencrantz and Guildenstern, since they so eagerly pursued his under Claudius' direction. And is it not now incumbent upon him, Hamlet continues, to also pay back the King for his evil deeds? Hamlet expresses his regret that he lost his temper with Laertes, whose grief and cause mirrors his own; he vows to "court his favors," and adds that Laertes' bravado has spurred his own resolve.

Osric enters with an invitation from Claudius to engage in a fencing match with Laertes, whose excellent qualities and skills are discussed at some length and agreed upon by Hamlet, Horatio, and Osric. Osric says Claudius has wagered substantial goods that Hamlet can beat Laertes, the duel to begin immediately if Hamlet is willing. Hamlet sends Osric to Claudius with his consent; a Lord returns at once, asking if Hamlet will engage Laertes now or later.

The duel is immediately arranged, with the King and Queen set to attend; Gertrude sends word to Hamlet to be courteous to Laertes before they begin duelling. Horatio predicts that Hamlet will lose, but Hamlet says he has been practicing and feels confident, despite a sense of misgiving "as would perhaps trouble a woman.". Horatio says if Hamlet has any misgivings at all, he will postpone the match and say Hamlet is "not fit." But Hamlet again expresses his belief in fate, and says "readiness is all;" whatever is meant to be will come sooner or later.

Claudius and Gertrude enter with the entourage attendant upon the fencing match, including Laertes, whom Claudius takes by the hand to Hamlet, urging reconciliation. Hamlet asks Laertes' pardon, attributing any offensive acts to his well-published madness. Laertes accepts the apology "in nature," but withholds total reconciliation until the opinions of his elders can verify that he will

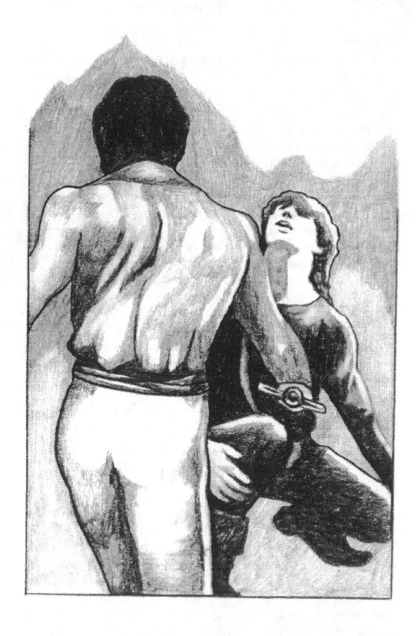

not diminish or relinquish his honor by making peace with Hamlet.

Claudius ascertains that Hamlet understands the wager, and Hamlet replies that Claudius has "laid the odds o' th' weaker side." Claudius admits this, but says it is only because Hamlet has improved. The pair take up foils; Laertes puts back the one Osric provides as "too heavy," and takes another. Claudius drops a pearl into a cup as added incentive for Hamlet, and says if Hamlet scores the first, second, or repays the third hit, the King will drink to him, which will signal the cannoneer to fire so that all will know of Hamlet's success.

After Hamlet's first "palpable hit," Claudius drinks, the cannons fire, and he urges Hamlet to drink; Hamlet, however, wishes to "play this bout first; set it by awhile." After the second hit, Gertrude drinks to Hamlet's success—from the poisoned cup, despite Claudius' attempts to stop her. As Laertes and Hamlet resume, they somehow exchange rapiers and are both wounded. Gertrude realizes she has been poisoned and dies; Hamlet orders the doors locked and the treachery sought out.

Laertes admits that the villainy "is here," and tells him they are both doomed, having been poisoned by the rapier, and that "the King's to blame." Hamlet then wounds Claudius with the "envenomed" point, and forces him to drink the rest of the poisoned cup and "Follow my mother." The King dies, Laertes and Hamlet forgive one another, and Laertes dies. Horatio intends to drink the rest of the cup, but Hamlet takes it from him and urges him "to tell [his] story."

Osric enters with news that Fortinbras has returned victorious from Poland. Hamlet endorses him as the next King of Denmark and then dies. Fortinbras and his retinue enter, and the Ambassador from England notes that it is too late for Claudius to thank them, that his commandment has been carried out, "That Rosencrantz and Guildenstern are dead." Horatio corrects the Ambassador: "He never gave commandment for their death." Horatio then orders the bodies placed "High on a stage" for public view, and vows to "Truly deliver" all the bloody and unnatural acts which have transpired to cause these deaths.

Fortinbras with sorrow sees that he now has the opportunity

to assume the Danish throne; Horatio hints that Hamlet spoke fa-
vorably to that issue, but urges the public ceremonies commence
"lest more mischance [on top of] plots and errors happen."
Fortinbras orders Hamlet's body carried "like a soldier" to the stage,
and says if Hamlet had had the chance, he would "have proved
most royal." He orders appropriate funeral rites for Hamlet, including the firing of ordnance, which ends the play.

Analysis

For four acts, Hamlet and Laertes have not met on stage, yet their lives have been closely intertwined. Hamlet's confusing and truncated relationship with Ophelia and his inadvertent murder of Polonius have made the two young men virtual enemies. Claudius has fanned the flame of Laertes' vengeance, even setting up the sword fight in which Hamlet is to be murdered. They finally meet in Act V, Scene 1, at Ophelia's graveside, where they struggle and proclaim their respective loves for the young maiden. But their reconciliation is foreshadowed several times. Hamlet asks Laertes, "What is the reason that you use me thus? I loved you ever"; and shortly thereafter he tells Horatio that he is "very sorry... That to Laertes I forgot myself," and that he plans to "court his favors." Later, Hamlet receives Gertrude's message to "use some gentle entertainment to Laertes before you fall to play," and Hamlet responds, "She well instructs me."

As they prepare to fence, Claudius takes Laertes' hand and puts it into Hamlet's, urging peace; Hamlet asks Laertes to pardon him, pleading madness. Of course, at this point, Laertes still intends to kill Hamlet, so the reconciliation is feigned. But as Laertes tells Claudius that this time he will score a hit against Hamlet, Laertes adds in an aside, "And yet it is almost against my conscience." And Gertrude's death evokes Laertes' confession to Hamlet: "Hamlet, thou art slain; ... The foul practice Hath turned itself on me ... Thy mother's poisoned ... The King, the King's to blame." As he dies, Laertes asks Hamlet to "Exchange forgiveness with me, ... Mine and my father's death come not upon thee, Nor thine on me!" Hamlet answers, "Heaven make thee free of it!"

There are several instances of irony in this act. For instance, Ophelia, almost certainly an innocent in this story fraught with betrayal and deceit, is denied a Christian burial because of the suspicious nature of her death. If her death were accidental, as it appears to be, she should have been given full holy rites. Everyone seems to love and want to protect Ophelia: Polonius, Laertes, Gertrude, Claudius—even Hamlet, though he denies it. His "get thee to a nunnery" speech suggests his desire to protect her from men, who are "arrant knaves all," not to be believed; no doubt he thinks primarily of Claudius, but also of himself, as he feigns his madness throughout the play.

At any rate, the pure maid must spend eternity "in ground unsanctified," presumably the fate shared by Polonius, Claudius, and Gertrude for their plottings. Perhaps Laertes and Hamlet will also lie in unsanctified ground for their deeds, unless their acts are done in the name of divine justice, a fine point which troubles Hamlet throughout the play. That she is killed by the "natural" world rather than by the political, which otherwise dominates the play, is further irony; she is done in by the world she claims as her own, shown most clearly by the flowers in her "mad scene."

Compounding her ultimate fate is Hamlet's admission at her funeral that he did love her more than "forty thousand brothers," despite his earlier protestations to the contrary. If Hamlet had not denied his love, perhaps she would not have gone mad, even at Polonius' death.

Laertes exhibits irony in his reluctance to fully accept Hamlet's apology, reconciling "in nature" only, "Till by some elder masters of known honor / I have a voice and precedent of peace / To keep my name ungored." Earlier, Laertes was bound to stop at nothing in seeking revenge against Claudius, whom he believed to have killed Polonius. At that time, Claudius urged Laertes to assemble his "wisest friends" to "hear and judge" whether Claudius bore any guilt. The irony is that Claudius, who urged delay and wise counsel, is guilty in principle; while Hamlet, who seeks forgiveness, is ultimately innocent—Polonius' death was accidental. In neither case is an impaneled "jury" likely to know the difference.

A final irony stems from the firing of the cannons in this act. Claudius sets up an elaborate system of signals, beginning with a toast to Hamlet's "hits," which will result in the firing of the cannons. But at the very end of the play, Fortinbras orders "soldiers' music and the rite of war" for Hamlet's passage, and orders, "Go, bid the soldiers shoot," and the stage directions indicate "a peal of ordnance" are to be shot off. What Claudius intended, in a perverse way as signals of Hamlet's success, serve at last as indication of Hamlet's death.

Just as the important events surrounding the Players' preparation and presentation of "The Mousetrap" are telescoped into a very short time frame (see Analysis for Act II), the events leading up to the sword fight are compressed. Claudius first suggests the duel to Laertes in Act IV, Scene 7. He counsels patience at Ophelia's funeral, indicating that their "last night's speech" will soon be put into action. In the next scene, Osric informs Hamlet of the King's wager, set for "immediate trial" if Hamlet agrees. He sends Osric back with his affirmative response, and a Lord returns to double check, and Hamlet again agrees to fight at once and sends the messenger back to Claudius. The royal party enters to witness the duel at line 226, and between lines 281 and 323, everyone has been mortally wounded; by line 358, Gertrude, the King, Laertes, and Hamlet are all dead. The sense of urgency is created by the increasingly brief interludes between events relevant to the duel.

When Laertes reveals to Hamlet that the treachery "is here" and that "No med'cine in the world" can save him, another motif is brought full circle: physical disease as manifestation of spiritual corruption. Evil has finally claimed everyone except Horatio (whom Hamlet barely prevents from committing suicide with the poisoned cup) and Fortinbras. The chain began with Claudius' murder of his brother in order to achieve the kingship, a political goal; and continued with Claudius' marriage to Gertrude, a personal prize.

In tandem, these two events precipitate those that follow: Polonius' death, Ophelia's madness and death, and the deaths of Rosencrantz and Guildenstern, Gertrude, Claudius, Laertes, and Hamlet. The Ghost's directive in Act I has finally been achieved. But for all of Hamlet's hesitation, the actual revenge on Claudius is almost incidental, certainly not a premeditated part of the duel.

That Fortinbras succeeds to the Danish throne is significant: like Hamlet, he was seeking to avenge his dead father, a king; but unlike Hamlet, he did not delay and sought to act almost at once. Only the wise counsel and constructive interference of his uncle prevented war with Denmark. As it happened, Fortinbras' entrance at the finale of the sword fight is perfectly timed, and he has both revenge and royalty at the play's conclusion.

Study Questions

1. Why is there debate surrounding the nature of Ophelia's funeral?

2. How long has the gravedigger been sexton, and when did he first become employed?

3. What joking insult to the English does Shakespeare put into the gravedigger's dialogue, regarding Hamlet's madness?

4. What cause does Laertes ascribe to Ophelia's madness, which led to her death?

5. What prompts Hamlet's outburst at Ophelia's graveside?

6. What order did Claudius' letter, carried by Guildenstern and Rosencrantz, convey to the English regarding Hamlet's fate?

7. How does Hamlet justify his counterfeit command that Rosencrantz and Guildenstern are to be murdered by the English?

8. In his apology to Laertes, what does Hamlet mean when he says, "I have shot my arrow o'er the house and hurt my brother"?

9. Why does Hamlet forbid Horatio to drink the rest of the poisoned cup?

10. Who will ascend to power as the new King of Denmark?

Answers

1. The issue is whether her drowning was accidental, in which case she may have a Christian burial—which the coroner has ruled, the gravedigger says; or whether it was intentional, in which case she may not have a Christian burial. Later, the Doctor of Divinity confirms that though "Her death was doubtful," the King has ruled that her burial be Christian. Thus, the gravedigger's supposition that nobility carries special privilege is probably true in this case.

2. The gravedigger has served as sexton for thirty years; he came the "day that our last king Hamlet overcame Fortinbras. . . . that very day that young Hamlet was born."

3. The gravedigger notes that Hamlet has been sent to England to "recover his wits," but adds that if he doesn't, it will not matter because "There the men are as mad as he."

4. Laertes blames Ophelia's madness on the "wicked deed," presumably her father's murder; he calls down a "ten times treble" curse on the killer, Hamlet.

5. He feels that Laertes is trying to outdo his own grief for Ophelia with all Laertes' rantings and his leaping into the grave. He leaps in as well, and says he'll "rant as well as [Laertes]."

6. For the good of both Denmark and England, they were to cut off Hamlet's head as soon as they had read the letter.

7. He tells Horatio that "they did make love to this employment." Their "baser natures" got caught in the sword play of "mighty opposites."

8. He means that his murder of Polonius was not "a purposed evil" and that he did not intentionally harm Laertes by his action, which Hamlet attributes to his own madness.

9. He wants Horatio to tell his (Hamlet's) story so that his name will be cleared rather than "wounded."

10. Fortinbras, whom Hamlet predicts will win the election; and Fortinbras himself remarks that he has some "rights of memory in this kingdom" which he plans to take advantage of, though he "with sorrow . . . [embraces his] fortune."

Suggested Essay Topics

1. Compare Claudius' use of the "arranged" fencing match between Laertes and Hamlet to Hamlet's use of "The Mousetrap," and his rewriting of the letters carried by Rosencrantz and Guildenstern.

2. Discuss the professions of love and grief expressed at Ophelia's funeral by Laertes and Hamlet, as compared to similar scenes featuring Claudius, in terms of their implications for the play's outcome: who is honest, deserving, and just, among the play's key players?

Sample Analytical Paper Topics

The following paper topics are based on the entire play. Following each topic is a thesis and sample outline. Use these as a starting point for your paper.

Topic #1

A pivotal scene in *Hamlet* is the "play within a play," designed to entrap Claudius. But many of the characters are "play-acting," and many other scenes echo the dominant theme of illusion and deceit. Trace the motif of acting, seeming, illusion, and deceit as opposed to sincerity, being, reality, and honesty, as these qualities are evidenced throughout the play.

Outline

I.   Thesis Statement: *Many of the characters in* Hamlet *are involved in duplicity designed to deceive, betray, or destroy others. The recurring motif of acting, seeming, illusion, and deceit as opposed to sincerity, being, reality, and honesty illustrates this underlying duplicity throughout the play.*

II. Act I

    A.   The sentinels debate whether the Ghost is real or "but our fantasy."

B. Hamlet tells Gertrude his grief is genuine: "I know not 'seems.'"

C. Laertes and Polonius both warn Ophelia that Hamlet's words and "tenders of love" toward her may be false.

D. The Ghost refers to Gertrude as "my most seeming-virtuous queen."

III. Act II

A. Polonius instructs Reynaldo to use indirection to learn how Laertes is comporting himself in Paris.

B. Rosencrantz and Guildenstern, and Polonius and Claudius are all trying to find out through devious means what is bothering Hamlet.

C. Hamlet notes the fickle nature of the populace, who once ridiculed Claudius, but who now pay dearly for his "picture in little."

D. Hamlet laments that he, who has cause, cannot avenge his father, while the actor is able to convincingly portray the emotions over imaginary characters and actions.

IV. Act III

A. Claudius and Polonius set Ophelia as bait to Hamlet, to try to learn the cause of his madness.

B. Claudius refers to the discrepancy between his deed and "[his] most painted word."

C. Hamlet instructs the Players to "hold, as 'twere, the mirror up to nature."

D. Hamlet is totally honest with Horatio about the Mousetrap plot because Horatio is beyond flattering, or being beguiled by falseness.

E. "The Mousetrap" and dumb show are "acting" or "seeming," and Hamlet's motive in having it performed is ulterior.

F. Hamlet tells Rosencrantz and Guildenstern that they are

"playing" him like a flute, and are not being honest with him.

G. Hamlet says his "tongue and soul in this be hypocrites" as he goes to speak with Gertrude, with whom he is very distraught.

H. Claudius discovers that his true thoughts cannot give way to his desired action of praying; yet Hamlet is fooled by the appearance of Claudius at prayer and does not murder him.

I. Hamlet tells Gertrude that her deeds have belied her vows; he urges her to "assume a virtue" if she does not actually have it.

V. Act IV

A. Claudius tells Gertrude of the necessity of making themselves appear blameless in Polonius' death.

B. Hamlet continues the pretense of madness as he teases Claudius about Polonius' corpse and his own departure for England.

C. Claudius reveals the fencing plot to Laertes, and says even Hamlet's mother will be convinced his death is an accident.

D. Claudius asks Laertes if he loved Polonius, "Or are you like the painting of a sorrow, / A face without a heart what would you undertake / To show yourself in deed your father's son More than in words?"

E. Claudius says they would be better off not to attempt the plot against Hamlet, since if it fails "And . . . our drift look through our bad performance."

VI. Act V

A. Hamlet and Horatio, discussing the similarity of all skulls despite the owner's station in life, says not even makeup can keep a lady from looking just like Yorick's skull.

B. Hamlet criticizes Laertes' show of grief as inferior to his own grief and love for Ophelia, and leaps into the grave also, so that his actions match his feelings.

C. Hamlet's use of his father's signet made the letters appear to be legitimate.

D. The sword fight appears to be legitimate, but is rigged against Hamlet's success.

Topic #2

Characters who parallel yet contrast one another are said to be *foils*. Authors often use foils to clarify character traits as well as issues in stories and plays. Discuss Shakespeare's use of foils, focusing on the parallels and contrasts of any one of these pairs of characters: Hamlet and Laertes; Hamlet and Horatio; Hamlet and Fortinbras; Laertes and Horatio; Claudius and Hamlet's father; Gertrude and Ophelia; Polonius and Claudius; Polonius and Hamlet.

Outline

I. Thesis Statement: *Shakespeare clarifies character traits as well as central issues in* Hamlet *by the use of foils, characters who parallel yet contrast one another. One such pair is* _____.

II. Hamlet and Laertes

A. Both men seek to avenge a father's death.

B. Both love Ophelia and mourn her death.

C. Laertes moves to seek immediate redress, while Hamlet hesitates.

D. Laertes is fooled by Claudius' duplicity, and endures Polonius' pomposity; Hamlet sees Claudius' treachery, and mocks Polonius.

III. Hamlet and Horatio

A. Hamlet praises Horatio as a just and temperate man, who "is not passion's slave," who suffers life's ups and downs with equanimity.

B. Hamlet is tormented, confused, and appears insane to nearly everyone who witnesses his behavior or hears him speak.

C. Although Horatio does not have the elements to contend with that Hamlet does, the suggestion is that Horatio would have responded very differently and more effectively, had he faced them.

IV. Hamlet and Fortinbras

A. Like Laertes, Fortinbras seeks immediate redress for his father's death, and is curbed only by the intervention of his uncle, King of Norway.

B. Hamlet must be prompted and later reminded by his father's Ghost to get on with the task of avenging the murder.

C. Hamlet's endorsement of Fortinbras as the new king of Denmark indicates Hamlet's approval of Fortinbras' character and demeanor.

V. Laertes and Horatio

A. Laertes is a lesser version of Horatio, made so because of Laertes' gullibility in the face of Claudius' manipulative flattery.

B. Hamlet notes that Horatio is above flattery, and thus unable to be manipulated.

C. Both young men are basically good and decent, and genuinely care for Hamlet and for the kingdom.

VI. Claudius and King Hamlet

A. Hamlet draws many invidious comparisons between these brothers, noting that Claudius is not one fraction the man he murdered.

B. Claudius attempts to manipulate everyone through deceit, which is apparently how he wooed Gertrude, who seems unaware of the fratricide until Hamlet reveals it to her.

    C. Claudius enlists the help of the British, under threat of retaliation if they do not kill Hamlet upon his arrival in England.

    D. Claudius ends up being directly or indirectly responsible for all of the deaths in the play: the King, Ophelia, Rosencrantz and Guildenstern, Gertrude, Laertes, Hamlet—and his own.

VII. Gertrude and Ophelia

    A. Both women are obedient to their men, Ophelia naively so.

    B. Both are knowing participants in plots to deceive Hamlet and learn the cause of his "transformation."

    C. Neither is fully aware of the evil directing her actions.

    D. Both try to humor Hamlet in his madness, seeking to gentle him out of his torment.

    E. Hamlet's rough treatment of them both results in Ophelia's eventual madness and Gertrude's repentance.

    F. Gertrude's characterization revolves around her sexuality; Ophelia's revolves around her chastity.

VIII. Polonius and Claudius

    A. Both men are arrogant and manipulative.

    B. Polonius is consistently shown to be a foolish old man who misjudges his abilities and popularity.

    C. Claudius is keenly aware of how he appears to others, and is at great pains to shore up public opinion to protect his regency.

    D. Hamlet says, when he mistakenly stabs Polonius, "I took thee for thy better" [Claudius].

IX. Polonius and Hamlet

    A. Polonius errs by acting too soon and too frequently in matters which are really not his concern.

B. Hamlet errs by delaying action in matters which are of central importance in his life and well-being.

C. Whereas Hamlet is perceived by nearly everyone as being insane, Polonius is widely regarded as a fool.

D. Hamlet's insanity is feigned; Polonius' foolishness is genuine.

Topic #3

Just as foils can help show similarities and differences between characters, parallel events can help clarify likenesses and contrasts between issues and characters' responses to them. Discuss Shakespeare's use of parallel plots and scenes throughout the play, showing their effects on characterization and thematic development.

Outline

I. Thesis Statement: *Shakespeare uses parallel plots and scenes in* Hamlet *to clarify and heighten similarities and differences between issues and the characters' responses to them.*

II. Sons avenging murdered fathers

A. Hamlet, Laertes, and Fortinbras are all sons seeking revenge for murdered fathers.

B.   The Player recites a scene at Hamlet's request depicting Pyrrhus' murder of Priam for the murder of Achilles, Pyrrhus' father.

III. Characters spying on one another

A. Polonius arranges for Reynaldo to spy on Laertes.

B. Claudius and Gertrude solicit the help of Horatio, then Rosencrantz and Guildenstern, then Ophelia, to spy on Hamlet.

C. Claudius and Polonius eavesdrop on Hamlet and Ophelia.

D. Polonius eavesdrops on Hamlet and Gertrude.

IV. Characters advising one another

    A. Polonius advises both Laertes and Ophelia.

    B. Both Laertes and Hamlet advise Ophelia.

    C. Claudius advises Laertes.

    D. Hamlet advises Gertrude.

V. The dumb show and Play re-enact the murder of the King by Claudius

VI. Ghost speaks only to Hamlet

    A. Act I: visible to the sentinels, but calls Hamlet aside to speak to him alone.

    B. Act III: invisible to Gertrude, still reserving speech only for Hamlet.

VII. Hamlet asks characters not to reveal information

    A. Hamlet makes the soldiers (Act I) swear not to tell what they have seen.

    B. Hamlet confides in Rosencrantz and Guildenstern that he is not really insane.

    C. Hamlet makes Gertrude promise not to reveal his pretended insanity.

Topic #4

Hamlet is often regarded as a play about an indecisive man, unable to take action. Explore the textual evidence for the various theories which attempt to explain Hamlet's inaction or delay in seeking revenge for his father's murder: lack of opportunity; too much thought and analysis; melancholy; Oedipus complex; doubt about the honesty of the Ghost; and doubts about his own ambitious motives.

Outline

I. Thesis Statement: *For many readers, Hamlet's seeming inability to avenge his father's death is the central issue of the play. His indecision is often cited as the "tragic flaw" which ultimately causes his death. Critics generally support one of six theories to explain Hamlet's inaction: lack of opportunity; too much thought and analysis; his melancholy; an Oedipus complex; his doubt about the honesty of the Ghost; and his doubts about his own ambitious motives.*

II. Lack of opportunity

  A. Hamlet is alone with virtually every other character except Laertes.

  B. When Hamlet is alone with Claudius, the King is at prayer, and Hamlet desists rather than send him to Heaven.

III. Too much thought

  A. Act II, Scene 2: Hamlet tells Rosencrantz and Guildenstern that "there is nothing either good or bad but thinking makes it so."

  B. Act III, Scene 1: Hamlet says, "conscience does make cowards of us all, / And thus the native hue of resolution / Is sicklied o'er with the pale cast of thought, and enterprises of great pitch and moment, with this regard their currents turn awry, and lose the name of action."

  C. Act IV, Scene 4: Hamlet debates whether his inaction is caused by "Bestial oblivion" or by "some craven scruple / Of thinking too precisely on th' event . . . "

IV. Melancholy

  A. Claudius urges Hamlet to snap out of his mourning, which he terms "obstinate condolement," and "unmanly."

  B. Hamlet soliloquizes, "But break my heart, for I must hold my tongue."

  C. Hamlet's apparent mood swings, which appear to onlookers as madness, would have been in keeping with symptoms of the ailment known as *melancholia*.

V. Oedipus complex

  A. Hamlet makes frequent references to how little time has passed between King Hamlet's death and Gertrude's remarriage.

    B.   Hamlet refers to Claudius as "dear mother," since "man and wife is one flesh."

    C.   Claudius now functions as Hamlet's father; in Oedipal terms, to kill Claudius would clear the path to Gertrude's bed.

    D.   Following Polonius' murder, Hamlet seems obsessed with the physical aspects of Gertrude's remarriage, and extracts her promise to abstain from Claudius' bed.

VI.   Doubt about the honesty of the Ghost

    A.   Act I: Hamlet asserts that "this vision here, / It is an honest Ghost."

    B.   Act II: He is uncertain—"The spirit that I have seen / May be a devil [who] abuses me to damn me."

    C.   Act III: He tells Horatio that Claudius' reaction to the Mousetrap will reveal if "It is a damned Ghost that we have seen."

    D.   Act III: When Claudius bolts, Hamlet confidently tells Horatio, "I'll take the Ghost's word for a thousand pound."

VII. Doubts about his own ambitious motives

    A.   Act III: Hamlet tells Ophelia that although he is moderately virtuous, "yet I could accuse me of such things that it were better my mother had not borne me: I am very proud, revengeful, ambitious. . . . "

    B.   Act III: Hamlet tells Rosencrantz that his "distemper" is because "I lack advancement," meaning that while Claudius occupies the throne, Hamlet cannot.

    C.   Hamlet tells Horatio that Claudius had "Popped in between th' election and my hopes, . . . " indicating that the Prince had anticipated being chosen by the people to succeed his father.

Topic #5

Authors often use physical weakness, disease, or deformity to symbolize or suggest mental, emotional, or spiritual illness or decay. Beneath the surface action of *Hamlet* runs an undercurrent of imagery of disease as opposed to healthfulness. Trace the motif of health and physical well-being as opposed to disease, illness, and weakness throughout the play. Show how Shakespeare links the physical symptoms with spiritual and political conditions.

Outline

I.   Thesis Statement: *Shakespeare uses imagery of disease, illness, and weakness to suggest physical, spiritual, or political illness or decay in* Hamlet.

II.   The idea of Hamlet's madness being caused by external events pervades the whole play.

III. Act I: When Hamlet follows the Ghost apart, Marcellus remarks that "Something is rotten in the state of Denmark."

IV.   Act III

   A. In his "To be, or not to be" speech, Hamlet notes that sleep/death would end the "heartache, and the thousand natural shocks That flesh is heir to!" (III, 1).

   B. Claudius tells Polonius that Hamlet's conversation with Ophelia did not seem to show either love or madness: "There's something in his soul O'er which his melancholy sits on brood, And I do doubt the hatch and the disclose Will be some danger; . . . "

   C. When, after the Dumb Show and aborted Play, Guildenstern tells Hamlet that Claudius is in "Marvelous [distemper]," Hamlet says it would make more sense to send for a doctor than for him, "for me to put him to his purgation would perhaps plunge him into more choler."

   D. He tells Rosencrantz that he cannot "Make you a wholesome answer; my wit's diseased".

   E. When Claudius explains his plan to ship Hamlet to England, Rosencrantz agrees: "The cess of majesty dies not alone, . . . Never alone did the King sigh, but with a general groan".

F. When Hamlet is unable or unwilling to kill the praying Claudius, opting for a time when Claudius' soul will be "damned and black As hell," he says, "This physic but prolongs thy sickly days".

G. As he chides Gertrude, Hamlet tells her that her unacknowledged, unconfessed "trespass . . . will but skin and film the ulcerous place / Whiles rank corruption, mining all within, Infects unseen".

H. Claudius, informed by Gertrude that Hamlet has murdered Polonius, says he erred in allowing Hamlet to remain at large, and "like the owner of a foul disease, to keep it from divulging, let it feed / Even on the pith of life"— thus reversing the image of insidious infection to apply to Hamlet's crime rather than to Gertrude's offense.

V. Act IV

A. In regard to the letter which Claudius sends to England, ordering Hamlet's murder, the King soliloquizes, "Do it, England, / For like the hectic in my blood he rages, / And thou must cure me".

B. When Gertrude unwillingly agrees to meet with "importunate, indeed distract" Ophelia, the Queen remarks on her own "sick soul (as sin's true nature is). . . . "

VI. Act V

A. As the sword fight is set to begin, Claudius explains how he will drink to Hamlet's health, which is the ultimate irony—having arranged for Hamlet's murder either by the sword or the cup.

SECTION EIGHT

Bibliography

Barnet, Sylvan, "Shakespeare: Prefatory Remarks," in William Shakespeare, *The Tragedy of Hamlet, Prince of Denmark*. Edward Hubler, ed. New York: Signet Classic, 1963 (viixx).

Boyce, Charles, *Shakespeare A to Z*, New York: Roundtable Press, 1990. "Hamlet," (231–234); "*Hamlet*," (234–241); "Quiney, Thomas," (529); "Shakespeare, William," (586–591).

Chute, Marchette, "Shakespeare, William," in *the New Book of Knowledge*, vol. 5 (17); Grolier, Inc., 1980. (130b–134).

Shakespeare, William, *The Tragedy of Hamlet, Prince of Denmark*. Edward Hubler, ed. New York: Signet Classic, 1963.